Basic
Psychic
Development

Basic Psychic Development

A User's Guide to Auras, Chakras & Clairvoyance

John Friedlander & Gloria Hemsher

York Beach, Maine, USA

First published in 1999 by
Weiser Books
P.O. Box 612
York Beach, ME 03910-0612
www.weiserbooks.com

Library of Congress Cataloging-in-Publication Data
Friedlander, John
    Basic psychic development : a user's guide to auras, chakras,
and clairvoyance / John Friedlander, Gloria Hemsher.
       p.   cm.
    Includes bibliographical references and index.
    ISBN 1-57863-023-1 (pbk. : alk. paper)
    1. Parapsychology. 2. Aura. 3. Chakras.
  4. Clairvoyance. I. Hemsher, Gloria. II. Title
  BF1272.F75   1999
  133.8—dc21   98-48101
                             CIP

EB
Typeset in 11 point Janson Text
Cover illustration is "John, Gloria, and Readers" by Anita
McKay, copyright © 1999.

Printed in the United States of America
06   05   04   03   02   01
9 8 7 6 5 4 3

Dedicated to

LEWIS BOSTWICK AND JANE ROBERTS

Contents

List of Figures

Acknowledgments

To our nonphysical teachers, Seth, Ruburt, Mataji, Yukteswar, Lahiri, Baba Muktananda, Babaji, Laxshmi, Saraswati, Purrball and Licker, who playfully engage us and help make life a joy.

With great respect and love to Gurumayi.

To all our friends, clients, and students who have been so helpful and encouraging.

To Gilbert Choudury, Lucy Duggan, Norma Gentile, Sue Remington, and Linda Sauernman for their careful reading and substantive suggestions.

To Ann Richer and April Schmidlapp whose many years of support of Basic Psychic Development classes provided an opportunity to hone the system.

To Anita McKay for her aura drawings and insight.

To the folks at Weiser for their patience, care and skill.

To Art Giser and Donna Ryen for their tireless support, insight and wisdom.

From Gloria: to my husband Gilbert Choudury for his tremendous support and for being mom when I wasn't there. To my son, Narayan, for his wit, computer wizardry and love. To my daughter, Sarah, for her sweet notes and hugs. To Elizabeth Meek, Rebecca Robinson, and Sue Remington for their faith in me and their loving support.

From John: to my wife, Pamela Moss, whose love and support has made my work possible.

Introduction:
Developing Your Intuitive/
Healing Vision

What are the attractions of *Basic Psychic Development?* They are heightened self-awareness, healing, and insights into our relationships. Share a recent conversation between the authors:

John: Hi Gloria, I had a very enlightening experience while giving a reading this morning. A client was telling me about some difficulties she was having with several men in her life.
Gloria (jokingly): Are you one of them!?
John: Well, I quickly became one. We were talking quite cordially and I was watching her aura. All of a sudden I noticed she was upset, there was a disturbance in her aura. Together we explored the nature of her concern and figured out that I had changed the direction of the conversation before she was comfortable. I was so grateful for the understanding and the opportunity to reconnect with her. Instead of my faux pas undermining our friendship, the whole interchange *increased* both our intimacy and our confidence. Being able to catch such clues in people's auras is just what I needed all my life.

The aura

Everyone has an aura. The aura is a bubble of spiritual light, sound, and feeling that surrounds each person. Through simple techniques and practices, you can learn to become more aware of both your own and other people's auras. As you explore your growing awareness the world becomes new, like the emerging world of a two-year old. Every day you can discover, understand, and interact more deeply with some aspect of your life that you couldn't even perceive the day before.

Auras are the wellspring of our physical, emotional, mental, and spiritual health. Our lives and relationships emerge out of the interaction between our own auras and the auras of others, and out of the interaction between our own auras and the inner energies of different spiritual dimensions of reality.

By developing your aura awareness, you can learn to heal the two major types of aura limitations: blockages and identity diffusion (boundary issues). *Basic Psychic Development* provides an integrated approach to removing blockages and clearing identity, which beginners and advanced practitioners both find life-changing. After establishing a secure foundation, *Basic Psychic Development* specializes in developing your ability to see auras. This ability, called *clairvoyance,* adds power to healing abilities, provides a path to connect with guides or angels, and eventually adds skills and intimacy to our daily interactions, to our relationships, to our lives.

Healing aura limitations

Two simple exercises will introduce you to the power you can utilize to heal the two kinds of aura limitations. The first deals with blockages, the second with identity clarification.

To remove a blockage from your aura, choose a past event that still causes you mild distress. Wait until you have the powerful specific techniques which come later in the book before healing a very distressing event; a mildly distressing event will do just fine for now. As you recall the event to your mind, sit comfortably straight and breathe freely. As you breathe in, draw all of the knowledge and wisdom to be gained from the experience out of the event and back into your body, mind, and aura. Whether you are able to identify the actual blockage in your aura at this point is not important. Just the intent to breathe in the knowledge and wisdom will help. Then, as you breathe out, breathe out any pain or confusion. Repeat the breathing cycle until you feel more at peace. The event may still be an unpleasant memory, but you will release much of the "stuckness"; you will be more free to move on.

You can repeat this exercise as often as is comfortable. Some experiences may require many repetitions over a period of weeks or months. Some will require the more integrated and specific approaches which come later in this book. Just the use of this single simple technique, however, can free up much of your spiritual power.

Exercise 1: *Breathing in the knowledge and wisdom*

1. Sit straight and breathe gently into your belly.
2. Recall a mildly distressing event.
3. As you breathe in, draw all of the knowledge and wisdom from the experience out of the event and back into your body, mind, and aura.
4. As you breathe out, exhale all the pain and confusion from the event.
5. Repeat the breathing cycle until you feel better and more comfortable with the event.

Breathing can also help you sort out your identity from others. Your aura is the ground of all your emotions and ideas. If your energy is in other people's auras (and theirs in yours), your identity is undermined, your emotions are faded and distorted, your ability to create your reality is impaired.

To help clear out your identity energy, imagine someone with whom you are entangled. Imagine them at a great enough distance that your respective energy bubbles (auras) have room to separate. As you breathe in, imagine that all of your identity energy that is trapped in the other person's aura is pulled back into your aura. As you breathe out, let all of the other person's identity energy that is trapped in your aura return to its owner. There are some people from whom you may never be entirely disentangled (such as parents, children, ex-spouses), but every little bit helps. Even more impressive results may come from using the integrated specific techniques that follow, but most people experience a remarkable success using just this simple breathing technique.

Exercise 2: *Clearing your identity energy*

1. Imagine someone with whom you are entangled. Place them far enough away from you so that your respective auras have room to separate.
2. As you breathe in, imagine all of your identity energy trapped in the other person's aura returning to you.
3. As you breathe out, let all of the other person's identity energy trapped in your aura return to them.

Amusement

Martial arts masters learn to maintain a balanced, open posture which allows them to be open to meet and respond to all of life—both to danger and pleasant opportunities. The emotional equivalent of this balanced, open position is a playful state we call *amusement*. Not surprisingly, different portions of the brain are used for psychic development than for, say, mathematics. It is easy to imagine that certain emotional orientations facilitate the use of the intuitive portions of the brain. Some emotions, such as seriousness, trigger stress hormones whose biological purpose is to narrow our attention and tighten our muscles in preparation for fight or flight. Amusement triggers other hormones that relax us and free our attention for social interchange. While both stress hormones and relaxation hormones serve useful purposes, the relaxing and freeing hormones generated by amusement help support psychic awareness.

The four relationships

To broaden the scope and effectiveness of your psychic development, we'll explore four unique and powerful psychic relationships. Building from the ground up, we'll begin with the unconditionally supportive relationship you have with the living Earth and the solar system, followed by the second relationship, your relationship to yourself (your chakras, and your past, present, and future). In the third relationship, we'll explore the evolving relationships you have with others. We'll conclude with the further opening of the loving relationship you have with your essence, your god of the heart.

Chapter One

The First Relationship:
Earth and Cosmic Energies

The first relationship we'll explore is the deeply loving and supportive relationship we each have with two vast entities—our living Earth and the cosmic energies. We'll begin with the powerful underpinning of our humanity—the nurturing and increasingly playful relationship we have with Earth.

The living Earth, with her space and time, provides us with what Lewis Bostwick[1] called our *kindergarten*,[2] our playspace. Earth ensures that our experience is distilled and simplified from infinite dimensions of the cosmos to the four dimensions of space/time.[3] Earth provides us with the loving structures that form the psychic kindergarten we live in, play in, and explore. It supports a three-dimensional space where we can grow and learn to become what Seth calls a conscious *cocreator* with God,[4] where we can learn to create our own reality, without having so much freedom that we're overwhelmed by our infinite possibilities.

---

[1]Lewis Bostwick (1918–1995), founder of The Berkeley Psychic Institute and source on which this presentation is primarily built.

[2]We think our understanding of kindergarten modifies Lewis' somewhat, but we think they are close.

[3]The three dimensions of space are length, width, and height. Space/time adds the dimension of time, making four dimensions in all.

[4]From conversations John had with Seth during the original Jane Roberts' Seth classes.

Our admission ticket to Earth's psychic kindergarten is our body. Psychically, our bodies reach deep into Earth, where they are nourished in unfathomable ways and grow out of Earth much like a tree. They are wondrous intuitive and emotional instruments that perpetually send and receive vital waves of energy and information, like a radio receiver/transmitter. Psychics have discovered that the body operates most capably and comfortably when "grounded," that is, when appropriately "tuned to" and aligned with Earth's frequency.

Grounding

Grounding balances and centers your body and allows you to feel safer, clearer, and supported. Being grounded enhances your ability to see, feel, and hear more deeply. Life seems to just flow more easily when your body is grounded.

You can ground yourself by creating a powerful energetic connection between your body and Earth called a *grounding cord*. Your grounding cord provides the unconditional support of the Earth's energy and allows you to align your body at an optimum frequency. It also provides a safe and powerful mechanism through which you can release excess and outdated energy from your aura.

In the first exercise, you create a grounding cord (an open "pipe" of light 3 to 6 inches in diameter) that extends from your pelvic area all the way down to and connected with the center of the planet. First, we'll discuss the varied aspects of grounding. Then, using the outline on page 8, you can practice it at your leisure.

Posture during meditations

In the past, many of the best meditation systems used a closed meditation posture, such as the famous lotus posture of the Buddha. That posture provided many benefits, but was directed at isolating the meditator from worldly relationships.

Since this meditation system embraces life's relationships, the most effective posture for practicing these techniques is an open posture. The posture called the Egyptian posture is an excellent open meditation posture. You sit comfortably in a chair, with your back straight, both feet flat on the floor, arms and legs uncrossed, and your hands resting, palms down, on your thighs.[5] In this posture, your energy can flow freely throughout your body and aura. It allows you to remain open to life, grounded in your body, and more in the moment (see figure 1, page 4).

You can be grounded regardless of your posture. The ideal is to be grounded all of the time,[6] whether you are sitting, walking, running, or flying. Once you become familiar with the process, you will find that you can easily ground while standing and moving through-out your day.

Breathing

Breathing gently, smoothly, and deeply into your belly during the exercises will increase their benefit and effectiveness. Shallow, rapid, or erratic breathing often indicates a need to increase your grounding.

Visualize your grounding cord as green

While you can ground yourself with other colors, we find that it is particularly effective for beginners to visualize their grounding cord as green.[7] The natural healing, calming, and earthy qualities of green contribute nicely to growth and grounding.

Initially, you will probably find it easier to visualize your grounding cord with your eyes closed. Eventually, you will be able to, and will want to, ground with your eyes open. You can imagine your grounding cord—see it, feel it, hear it, or

---

[5]When grounding, most people find it helpful to let the palms rest on the thighs, facing downward, although for most meditations, the palms should face up.

[6]Except when intentionally channeling.

[7]After a time, you'll spontaneously ground on whatever energy color is appropriate for you.

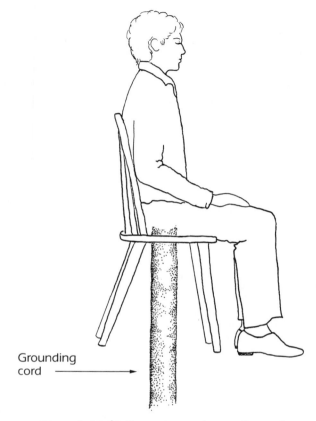

Grounding
cord

Figure 1. Meditation posture and grounding cord.

intend it—looking somewhat like a green fiber-optic tube or
an open pipe of green light. [8]

The chakras used in grounding

The grounding exercise will introduce you to three important
energy centers in your body: your first chakra, your third

---

[8]Each person will perceive colors in his or her own unique way. Some
will "see" little or nothing. Instead of seeing, some may feel or hear their
perceptions; others may smell or taste them. Most see, hear, feel, or simply
"know." Recognize, validate and hone your natural perceptions. With practice the other methods of perception will grow.

chakra, and your foot chakras. *Chakras* are dynamic psychic organs, confluences of vital energies that are received, transmitted, and metabolized in your body and aura. They often appear as two cones of energy, connected to and emerging from the spine, one forward and one backward. The chakras have numerous qualities attributed to them. In the beginning, you will be working with the aspects of each of these three chakras that ground you and facilitate the energy flow into and throughout your body and aura[9] (see figure 2, page 6).

The chakra that you ground from is called the first chakra. This psychic organ facilitates your bringing grounding energy into your body and aura from Earth. In this system, the first chakra is placed differently for women than for men. For women, the first chakra is located between the ovaries; for men, it is located in its traditional site, at the base of the spine. Placing the first chakra a little higher on the spine for women allows them to run their bodies at a higher frequency. This seems to be a more natural female level.[10]

The third chakra is located at the solar plexus, just a little below where the ribs come together in the abdomen. This chakra facilitates the distribution of the various energies throughout your body and aura.

Facing downward in the arches of the feet are the foot chakras. The foot chakras allow you to effortlessly bring Earth energy directly into your body.

How to create a grounding cord

You create your grounding cord by first imagining a spinning ball of earthy-green light anywhere from 3 to 6 inches in diameter in your first chakra. Let it spin (the direction of spin doesn't matter), then let it fall through your chair. As it falls, imagine that it creates an open tube of green light behind it, similar to the tail of a comet. Allow it to fall effortlessly all the

---

[9]An in-depth discussion of the seven major chakras and their specific qualities will be found in chapter 2.

[10]This explanation was given by friend and clairvoyant Donna Ryen.

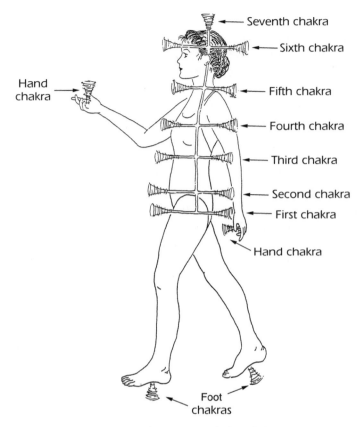

Seventh chakra

Sixth chakra

Hand chakra

Fifth chakra

Fourth chakra

Third chakra

Second chakra

First chakra

Hand chakra

Foot chakras

Figure 2. The major "in-body" chakras.

way down to the center of the planet. You may enjoy imagining gravity as a form of love that gently pulls your grounding cord down to Earth's center for you. When it reaches the Earth's center, let the ball expand and merge with Earth's energy. Allow Mother Earth to greet you with a warm embrace and to align your body to just the right frequency for life on our planet.

The larger the diameter of your grounding cord, the more grounded you will be. To facilitate an increased grounding capability, once you've established your grounding-cord connetion, allow it to expand to 6 to 10 inches in diameter, or to whatever size feels appropriate and comfortable for you. Check to see that your grounding cord is securely connected to your first chakra, and unobstructed and unbroken all the way down to its connection to the center of the planet.

Your grounding cord will help regulate energy flow

You may find it beneficial to intend that any excess or out-dated energy in your aura will automatically flow down your grounding cord. Your grounding cord, much like the grounding wire in an electrical circuit, helps keep your body safe and comfortable, never running more energy than is appropriate for you at any time.

Advanced student: I'd had deep meditations for many years but never quite knew how to carry them into my day. Soon after arriving at work I would be just as harried as everyone else. "Let go" was the advice I'd get. I'd wonder, "Let go to *where?*" When I learned how to ground myself, it seemed apparent to me that I had probably never been "grounded" a day in my life. It felt great. Grounding made it so much easier to stay centered. And the first time I released that "nervous" energy down my grounding cord I understood what it meant to "let go."

Bringing Earth energy in through your feet

Once you've established your grounding cord, you will want to bring the nourishing Earth energy up into your body. You can allow fresh green Earth energy to flow effortlessly up into your foot chakras, through your calves, knees, and thighs, then up the front of your body and into your third chakra (your solar plexus, where your ribs come together). Next, you'll see, feel, hear, or imagine the fresh Earth energy energizing your third chakra for a moment. Allow the nourishing energy to flow out into your entire body, mind, and aura. You can bring as much fresh Earth energy into your body as you like.

Allow any excess or undesirable energy that you are ready to release from your body and aura to simply flow down your grounding cord. Earth will neutralize and recycle it for you.

Establish a comfortable proficiency

With a little practice, you'll be able to ground in about ten seconds or less. While familiarizing yourself with the specifics, you can expect your practice sessions to take up to ten minutes. Since grounding is the foundation for every technique in this system, you may want to establish a comfortable proficiency with the process before proceeding on to the subsequent exercises. To keep pace with your growth, release your grounding cord (letting it dissolve back into the Earth) and create a new one each time you meditate or make any big changes.

Exercise 3: *Grounding*

1. Sit Egyptian style in a chair.
2. Breathe gently and deeply into your belly.
3. Close your eyes and imagine a ball of spinning green light, from 3 to 6 inches in diameter, in your first chakra. Then allow it to spin a little faster still.
4. Let the ball drop effortlessly all the way down to Earth's center and create a grounding cord for you.
5. Allow the ball to expand and merge with the Earth's core.
6. Feel yourself more secure, more at ease, more playful and aligned with the Earth's frequency.
7. Let your grounding cord expand to 6 to 10 inches in diameter, or to whatever size feels comfortable to you.
8. Let fresh green Earth energy flow up into your foot chakras, through your legs, then up the front of your body and into your third chakra.
9. See, feel, hear, or imagine Earth's nurturing energy in your third chakra for a moment, then allow it to

flow out into every cell of your body, mind, and aura.

10. Check your grounding cord to see that it is securely connected to your first chakra, and unbroken and unobstructed all the way down to the Earth's center. Make adjustments if necessary.

11. Bring as much fresh Earth energy into your body and aura as you wish.

12. Give your body permission to release any excess or unwanted energy down your grounding cord.

13. Remind yourself that, henceforth, your grounding cord will continue to operate, setting your body at your Earth frequency, bringing fresh Earth energy into your body as needed, and releasing unwanted or excess energy as well.

14. When finished, stand up and stretch.

Being in the center of your head

We find another powerful technique that can assist you in grounding is bringing your awareness into the *center of the head*. The center of the head, often called *the seat of the soul*, is a very calm and lovely energy found in and around the pineal gland.[11] While there are slight individual variations, the center of the head can be found roughly between, and about as high as the top of the ears (see figure 3, page 10). Resting your awareness in the center of your head helps you focus your body and mind in the present and increases your clarity and neutrality as well.[12]

Take a moment now to locate and become familiar with the feel of having your awareness in the center of your head.

---

[11]Though the center of the head is really part of the fourth relationship to be covered in this book, not the first, it is a skill that is useful from the beginning.

[12]Neutrality, a state of being open to your experiences, is a key component in the development of your clairvoyance. It is discussed at length in chapter 6.

Figure 3. *The center of the head.*

For some people, placing their hands over their ears makes it easier to find. There are no rules, just exploration.

Advanced student: I just play with my awareness, shifting it back and forth in the general location of the pineal gland until it "feels" good. When I reach a certain calmness, I know I'm in the center of my head.

Exercise 4: *Finding the center of your head*

1. Relax, and breathe gently and deeply into your belly.
2. Ground, or check your grounding.
3. Playfully notice where your awareness is.

4. Bring your awareness into the center of your head, and explore how that feels.
5. Allow your awareness to rise to the ceiling for a moment and explore how that feels.
6. Invite your awareness into the center of your head.
7. Practice letting your awareness rise to the ceiling and bringing it back in until you feel reasonably familiar with the energy in the center of your head.
8. Conclude your exploration by allowing your awareness to rest in the center of your head.

Bringing your awareness to the center of your head is a progressive exploration. You will continue to discover its subtlety, but even your first efforts will heal previously hidden levels of your being. From now on, you can bring your awareness to the center of your head whenever you ground, or anytime you want increased effectiveness and clarity.

Owning the Room

Every exercise in this book will begin with grounding and the following technique, owning the room. This exercise, though simple to do, has very deep ramifications. Owning the room develops and enhances your appreciation of the fact that the universe has provided you a personal space in which to flourish. Owning the room develops and enhances your appreciation of the fact that you are entitled to thrive, and that you are completely supported in your growth.

What makes this exercise so exceptional is that, when you own a room psychically, you acknowledge, validate, and own it from your unique frequency, your unique self. Others can own the same room at the same time from their own unique frequency. You are not in competition with or in violation of anyone else's right to their unique space. You are understanding, seeing, feeling, hearing, and validating that you have a right to thrive. You have a right to be safe and be supported, as do others.

The universe wants you to make your unique impact. Through you, the universe, or God, knows itself by your uniqueness. In owning the room, you are claiming your own uniqueness and allowing others theirs. It could be said that you are not owning space, so much as owning your own uniqueness which we call owning the room.

There's an important but subtle difference between occupying a room with your energy and owning it from your unique frequency. You own the room with your intent, without filling it with your energy. If you filled the room with your energy, you *would* be in competition[13] with others. Owning a room is an abstract process. While doing the exercise, you can affirm for yourself—see, feel, or hear—that you are where your uniqueness will bloom. While the exercise does change the quality of the energy in the room, the change is simply one of validating the universal permission given to you by All That Is to learn, to explore, to grow, to engage the cosmic dance of life.

Exercise 5: *Owning the room*

1. Resting your awareness in the center of your head, breathe gently and deeply into your belly and ground yourself.
2. Imagine sending a thin green line out from each foot to the four corners of the floor.
3. Affirm silently to yourself, "My floor," as you own the floor from your unique frequency.
4. From just above your head, send a thin golden line out to each corner of the ceiling.
5. Affirm silently to yourself, "My ceiling," as you own the ceiling from your unique frequency.
6. Own the entire room; floor to ceiling, front to back, and side to side.

---

[13]Competition is a term used by psychics in a spiritual way. It refers to psychic energies that are in conflict.

7. Affirm silently to yourself, "My room."
8. Release any excess or old energy from your aura, and replenish your aura with fresh Earth energy.
9. Check your grounding.
10. When ready, stand up and stretch.

Owning the room is not the same as owning your space

Owning the room is accomplished with your intent, not with your energy. In addition to owning the room, we'll introduce another concept later in the book that we refer to as owning your space. Owning your space is equivalent to owning your aura. To own your space or aura, you do own it with your energy, because it's you. It's who you are. The space you "own" in a room is not "who" you are, but a permissive space where you can grow and thrive.

You can own the room wherever you are

You can use this tool in imaginative ways to own the room wherever you are by your intent; out in the middle of a field, flying in an airplane, driving in your car. You don't literally need a room. You can own your right to thrive as a human being anywhere you are.

One student credits the technique with having helped her overcome an incapacitating fear of driving. She created a safe and supportive environment for driving by first grounding and then owning the room for a space surrounding her car. Then she'd ground and own her car. Within six weeks, she had released her fears about driving. Soon after, her career changed and she has since found herself on the road quite a lot.

You may wonder whether you can own the room once and for all, whether you can create it and carry it with you throughout the day. Theoretically you can, but, in practical terms you will find it beneficial to recheck your ownership in each physical space where you spend time. Other people may be consciously or unconsciously competing with you in the new space. Grounding and owning the room will facilitate your own clarity.

Advanced student: I work as a medical records clerk in a high security prison. It's a massive cement and steel structure, a football field long, with 500 people. Talk about "rage" energy. I have to pass through a cell block of heavy offenders to get to my office, which sits above a cell block of about 300 inmates. I'm very sensitive, so I am glad to have learned how to ground, own the room, and clean my aura. It's given me a greater feeling of stability, especially in my lower chakras. I still am affected, but I don't get thrown around by the energy as much anymore. When I go home, I run energy and clean my aura, which helps me bounce back. I can leave their rage behind.

Running Earth and Cosmic Energy

As you will see, each technique in this book builds on the preceding one, very much like a train gaining momentum. If the only kind of energy you ever ran were Earth energy, you would become too grounded, unable to move. So, to balance the flow of energy in your body, you want to mix Earth energy with cosmic energy.

Golden cosmic energy

Just as Earth's energy is unconditionally supportive of your explorations, so too is the energy available to you from the universe. Though universal energy exists in infinite vibrations and colors, it is good while learning to use a lovely golden universal or cosmic energy, because of its open, neutral, and responsive qualities.[14] Imagine cosmic energy as coming from or through the Sun, and as having a molten golden light or feeling. When bringing cosmic energy into the aura we'll refer to it as bringing in golden suns or running cosmic energy.

---

[14]You might wonder why we don't use white light. White light, which carries all the frequencies, is really too high a frequency for you to run through your body and be in your body. When it runs through your body, your personal awareness will float above the body.

Using your crown chakra to run energy

We now introduce the crown chakra into the next stage of running energy. The crown chakra, which faces upward on the top of the head, facilitates bringing cosmic energies into your body and aura from above. As you begin to work with the two energies (Earth energy and cosmic energy), please note that all descending energy flows down the *back* channels, while all ascending energy flows up the *front* channels of your body.

Basic method for running Earth and cosmic energy

To put it all together, first ground, then own the room and allow Earth energy to flow up through your foot chakras, up through your knees and thighs and into your first chakra. Bring the cosmic energy into your aura through your crown chakra. Allow the cosmic energy to flow through your crown chakra and down your back into your first chakra. In the first chakra, let the Earth and cosmic energies mix. Bring that mixture up the front of your body and into your third chakra (at the solar plexus). From there, allow the mixture to flow out, bathing your entire body, mind, and aura.

Perceiving the two different energies is an individual experience. For those of you who are visual, it will be easy: the Earth energy will be green and the cosmic energy will be golden. For those who hear energy, the two energies will sound different. For those who feel energy, the two energies will feel quite different. You can consider yourself psychic when you can perceive the difference between two psychic energies, any two. It's like learning how to read. As a first grader, you can read. You may not know how to read very well, but your reading process is essentially the same as an advanced reader. Building on your basic reading skill, your ability to read will change and grow. Similarly, when you can distinguish between two different kinds of energies, you can consider yourself to be psychic. Building upon that simple start, your abilities will grow rapidly.

You may want to run no more than seven cycles of this mixture per sitting for the first week or so. You have always been running energy, even before these techniques. But when you first begin to intentionally direct your energy, you tap into an unaccustomed power. You may tend to breathe more deeply and, while that is good, your body must have the time it needs to adjust. Quite rapidly, you will proceed to longer meditations where you will run much more energy. If you pay attention to what's happening in your mind and body while meditating, remaining playful and doing the techniques because they are fun, you will be fine.

The point is to run appropriate energy in appropriate amounts. Remind yourself that your grounding cord is always venting off any excess energy, as well as any energy that you no longer need or desire.

Fill the cleared portions of your aura with fresh energy

In this next exercise, and from now on, when you release outdated or undesired energy from your aura, fill the newly cleared space with a mixture of fresh Earth and cosmic energy. Not only will that replenish your aura, it will help you "own" that portion of your aura.

Reversing polarities

Whenever you run cosmic energy, finish by bending over and "spilling" any excess energy out of your crown. This will help keep the energies balanced and avoid any excess cosmic energy having to go all the way through your body before going out your grounding cord. This motion, called "reversing polarities," is also a great way to loosen up your back after doing energy work.

Exercise 6: *Basic method for running Earth and cosmic energy*

1. Breathing gently and deeply into your belly, come into the center of your head.
2. Ground and own the room.

3. From the Earth's center, bring a 10-inch ball of fresh green energy up into your foot chakras, and roll it up your legs into your first chakra.
4. Take a moment to see, feel, or hear that energy.
5. From above your head, bring a golden sun in your crown chakra, then roll it down your back into your first chakra.
6. See, feel, or hear those energies as they mix.
7. Bring the mixture up the front of your body and into your third chakra, at your solar plexus.
8. From your third chakra, allow the mixture to expand and fill your entire body, mind, and aura.
9. Release any excess or outdated energy, and replenish your aura.
10. Check to see that you are still grounded and owning the room.
11. When you are ready, stand up, stretch, and reverse polarities.

Pace yourself and pay attention to your body's signals

You will begin to make considerable changes in your energy field with this powerful exercise. If you ever feel light-headed after this, or any meditation, wiggle your fingers and toes, pat your body, and use all your senses. From a seated position, you can bend over and reverse polarities. Check your grounding, and breathe gently and deeply into your belly. You may want to bring in more Earth energy. Washing your hands and drinking some water helps you feel your body. Pace yourself and pay attention to your body's signals. There's no hurry. Big changes will happen even with small efforts.

Pain

When a person's energy is moving, he or she is growing. Wherever a person's energy is stopped, he or she will experience pain. Pain is felt where energy has stopped flowing. A straightforward way through any pain is to become more attuned and grounded, so that you can run your energy clearly and smoothly.

Advanced method for running energy

If you have practiced grounding and running energy for a week or two, you may now be ready to move on to the more advanced method. The advanced technique for running energy builds upon the previous exercises in two ways: it creates continuous flows of Earth and cosmic energy into your body, and it provides a more sophisticated method for dispersing the mixture of Earth and cosmic energy throughout your entire body, mind, and aura.

First, establish a continuous flowing loop of Earth energy. Bring Earth energy from the center of the Earth up through the ground into your foot chakras, then allow it to flow up your legs, into the bottom of your first chakra, then back down your grounding cord to the center of the planet. This will create a perpetual loop, a continuous flow of unconditionally supportive and nurturing Earth energy for your body to use at all times (see figure 4, page 19).

Similarly, bring a continuous flow of cosmic energy into your crown chakra, down your back, through the top of your first chakra and back up the front of your body. When you bring the stream of cosmic energy down your back and through the top of your first chakra, you allow the stream to pick up and mix with a little of the Earth energy, so that the ratio is about 10 percent Earth energy, 90 percent golden cosmic energy.[15] Then bring that mixture up the front of your body, but, instead of bringing it into your third chakra, allow it to continue to flow through your third chakra and up to your shoulders. Without breaking the flow, allow one

---

[15]The percentage will vary from person to person depending upon their ethnicity, age, skill, and a host of other factors, which will emerge eventually with one's growing awareness. For example, Lewis Bostwick used to say that ethnic Native Americans run more Earth energy than any other group on the planet.

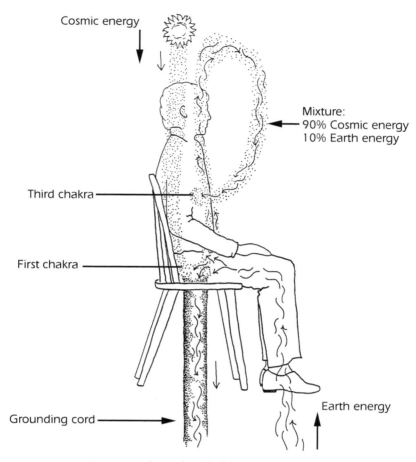

Figure 4. *Advanced method for running energy.*

third of the mixture to move down your arms and out your hand chakras. The remaining two-thirds of the energy continues upward to your crown. From your crown chakra, simply allow the energy to fountain up a foot or more out of your crown, and then to flow forward and down to your third chakra. Your third chakra will then automatically disperse the nourishing energy throughout your entire body, mind, and aura.

Exercise 7: *Advanced method for running Earth and cosmic energy*

1. Breathing gently and deeply into your belly, bring your awareness into the center of your head.
2. Ground, allowing Earth energy to flow into your foot chakras, up your legs, into the bottom of your first chakra, then back down your grounding cord to the center of the planet, establishing a continuous flow.
3. Own the room from your unique frequency.
4. Spend a moment to see, feel, or hear the continuous and playful flow.
5. From above your head, bring a golden sun into your crown chakra, allow it to flow down your back and into the back of your first chakra.
6. Let those energies mix in a ratio of 10 percent Earth energy to 90 percent cosmic energy. (Allow the remaining 90 percent of the Earth energy to continue its flow back down to the Earth's center, and then back up with a little new energy in the perpetual loop.)
7. Bring the mixture all the way up the front of your body to your shoulders. Without breaking the flow, allow one third of the mixture to move down your arms and out to your hand chakras. The remaining two-thirds of the energy continues upward to your crown. From your crown chakra, allow the energy to continue up a foot or more above your crown, then to spill forward and down into your third chakra.
8. Let your third chakra automatically disperse the nourishing energy throughout your entire body, mind, and aura.
9. Release any excess or outdated energy down your grounding cord and replenish your aura.
10. Check that you are still grounded and owning the room.

11. When you are ready, stand up, stretch, and reverse polarities.

Falling asleep during meditation (resistance)

When people first start running energy, they sometimes report that they feel like falling asleep. Though it may be that they *are* physically tired, it's more likely that they are encountering various kinds of resistance. Running energy often lights up, that is, awakens resistance or concerns that are held in our auras. Exploring resistance and concerns usually unearths a wealth of information about who you are allowed to be, and how much you might be allowed to know. With practice, you will become more adept at recognizing what those concerns might be for you. Listen and treat any concerns with respect. Your resistance is invaluable in what it will teach you.

Validate your resistance

If you recognize a resistance, first congratulate yourself on the recognition, and then "say hello" to it, that is, acknowledge and validate it (see Saying hello and validating your perceptions, page 22). Explore your resistance. Communicate with it and ask what its concerns are. Say to yourself, "Okay, I have a tendency to fall asleep when I run energy. What is its origin?" You may get answers that surprise and even liberate you, like discovering an energy in your aura that disagrees with your conscious desires. Some energies may resist your opening up your intuition or your learning how to be self-empowered. As you explore resistance, those barriers will fall. Sometimes simple recognition of the source will suffice. Sometimes you will need the more powerful tools you will find later in this book.

In the meantime, there are several techniques that can help you stay awake and aware. Sit straighter in your chair, roll your eyes up in your head, place your hands over your ears (which helps you come into the center of your head more easily). You can also imagine a brightness in the center of your head, open your eyes, and/or breathe more deeply, extending your exhalation two counts longer than you would otherwise exhale.

Saying hello and validating your perceptions

To say hello to something—a resistance, an emotion, a chakra, an energy—is to simply validate it and let it become "real." It's a way of attending to it, recognizing and allowing your body to say, "Oh, that's what exists, at least according to my perceptions and interpretations right now."

There's an important subtlety in validating your perceptions. Validating your perceptions and interpretations doesn't mean that they are true, it just means that they are yours for that moment. Part of validating your perceptions and interpretations requires that you realize that they may be different from moment to moment. For example, as we learn something new, we often need to adjust our old interpretation to our new understanding. You can't truly validate your perceptions and interpretations if you demand that they be constant, unchanging, and unyielding. It is our opinion that the only way to truly validate your perceptions and interpretations is to be aware of the fact that they change from moment to moment. Saying hello to your perceptions is simply saying, "This is what I perceive and believe in this moment," and saying hello to someone else's emotions is saying to yourself, without judging the other, "That is what you perceive and believe in this moment."

Suggestions for Further Explorations

1. Explore grounding your environment. With your intent ground your car, your office, your computer, lost keys, etc.
2. Notice what "being grounded" and "owning the room" feels like in your busy world. Remember that you can be amused. Notice what it feels like when you are not grounded and not owning your room. Then ground and own the room again.

3. Notice where your consciousness is throughout the day and, if you find it drifting, with amusement invite it back into the center of your head.
4. Before going to sleep, spend at least five to ten minutes grounding, running energy, owning the room, and saying hello to your body and aura.

Chapter Two

The Second Relationship: Yourself, Your Chakras, and Your Pictures

The first relationship, your relationship with the Earth and the cosmos, and your fourth relationship, your relationship with your essence (see chapter 4), secure you in transcendent or archetypal relationships, affirming a place and a relationship with All There Is. The second and third relationships directly explore your individual personal life and relationships. In the second relationship, two concepts, chakras and energy blocks or pictures, are explored in depth. They will be combined, with each other and other concepts and techniques, into an adventure in personal growth. Each concept and technique refines your understanding of the others.

Chakras

Chakras are the psychic organs where the essential energies for your emotional, physical, and spiritual health are received, transmitted, metabolized, and utilized. Each chakra has its own unique focus, allowing specific categorizations of your psychic perceptions (see Table 1, page 26). The term *chakra* is a Sanskrit word meaning "cyclone" and, quite befittingly, these dynamic energy centers are often seen as swirling cones of energy. They are also frequently experienced as colors, discs, cylinders, and flowers. Through meditation you can learn to see, feel, or hear your chakras, and often you can learn to see, feel, or hear the chakras of others as well.

Table 1. The Chakras at a Glance

Chakra	Location	Function
Foot	Arch of the feet	Receiving Earth Energy
Hands	The center of each palm	Giving, Receiving, Expressing, Healing
First	Base of the spine for men, between the ovaries for women	Grounding, Survival
Second	Three fingers below navel	Emotions, Boundaries
Third	Solar plexus	Understanding, Energy Distribution, Ego
Fourth	Center of chest	Community, Love
Fifth	Notch of throat	Communication, Inner Identity, Telepathy
Sixth	Center of the head	Clairvoyance, Intellect, Beliefs
Seventh	Crown of the head	Knowingness, Wisdom,

There are seven major chakras along your spine, as well as the lesser-known but still vital chakras of your feet and hands[1] (see figure 2, page 6). As you read about each

---

[1]There are actually thousands of chakras, both inside and outside of the body. The major out-of-body chakras are discussed in chapter 8, page 123.

individual chakra, please take a moment to familiarize yourself with its location. Grounding, owning the room, and running a little energy will increase your ability to see, feel, or hear them. Energize your hands by shaking them out and rubbing them together for a moment. Begin to notice the flow of energy in your hands, particularly in your palms. Allowing that your perceptions may be very subtle at first, hold your hand out about three inches in front of each chakra location and practice feeling, seeing, hearing, or imagining the energy there. Try finding another person's chakras by placing your hands out in front of the different chakra locations and sensing each chakra's energy. Validate your perceptions, however subtle, and your perceptions will continue to grow.

The foot chakras: opening to Earth energy

There are numerous chakras in your feet. In this system, the particular chakras you will utilize for opening to Earth energy are in the arch of each foot. They are swirling cones of energy facing downward.

In the past, to meditate and to ground, a meditator sat in the lotus position, the posture in which the Buddha is usually portrayed. Now, in the Aquarian Age (the New Age), newly important chakras in the feet provide us with a more potent way of opening to Earth energy. This leads to a new mobility, allowing us to walk around and be in the world while running powerful psychic energies.

The hand chakras: healing

There are also many chakras in the hands. You can imagine your hand chakras as swirling cones of energy in the palm of each hand. Receiving from the world, expressing and creating in the world, your hand chakras are vital centers of healing.

The first chakra: grounding and survival

Your first chakra is often called the survival chakra because of its role in facilitating our physical needs and feelings of security. In this system, as introduced earlier with the grounding exercise, the first chakra is placed at the base of the spine for men and between the ovaries for women. Imagine your first chakra as two cones of swirling energy emerging from the spine, one facing forward, the other facing backward. Your first chakra allows you to align your body with the frequency of the planet and sustain your grounding. It sets your individually correct frequency for the planet Earth and provides the mechanism through which your hopes, dreams, and desires, both conscious and unconscious, both recognized and unrecognized, are manifested. It's your membership chakra; it allows you to be a member of the planet Earth.

The second chakra: appropriate boundaries

You can imagine your second chakra as two cones of swirling energy joined at the spine, located about three finger widths below your navel, one cone facing forward, the other facing backward. Many systems place the second chakra at the pubic bone. At the pubic bone, one accesses powerful subconscious sexual energies and, of course, there is a very important chakra there. The higher placement used in this system focuses on emotions and appropriate boundaries, though it still includes the pleasurable and psychically creative energies of sex.

The second chakra is the most problematic chakra for developing psychics, because the second chakra is where you literally feel other people's energy, where you actually let other people's energy into your space. A lot of psychics "read" from their second chakra, bringing other people's energy into their space, and feeling and seeing that energy inside of themselves. That style is discouraged in this system. It can be an unhealthy way to do a reading. As you explore your chakra system and aura, you will learn to recognize what is you and what is not, thereby learning how to recognize and honor psychic boundaries.

The third chakra: understanding yourself and others

Your third chakra is located at the solar plexus, just below where the ribs come together. Again, one energy cone faces forward, the other backward, with both connected at the spine. The third chakra is often called the ego or power chakra. At its best, the third chakra provides a refined understanding of yourself and others. It also acts as a psychic energy pump for your aura, much like the heart acts as a blood pump for the physical body.

The third chakra is the chakra that most of us abuse by trying to control life, misunderstanding power and ego. Everyone is supposed to have an ego, just as they're supposed to have a body. With maturity, our egos relinquish trying to control others and confine themselves to understanding ourselves and others. Using this understanding, we can set our own course and collaborate with others.

The fourth chakra: love and community

There are lots of chakras in the chest area. In this system, we place the fourth chakra in the center of the chest. Again, imagine two cones of energy facing opposite directions, connecting at the spine. The fourth chakra is known as the heart chakra, the chakra of love. Ideally, the fourth chakra is where you engage in community, in relationships. Its appropriate functioning requires a mature individuation built through the energies of the three lower chakras. With the lower chakras functioning properly, you have a foundation to be a fully individuated human being, and to be fully connected to and in relationship with others. The fourth chakra is where your spirit connects with your body.

The fifth chakra: communication and telepathy

The fifth chakra is located at the notch at the base of the neck. It also appears as two swirling cones of energy, facing opposite directions and connected at the spine. The chakra of subtle vibration and sound, your fifth chakra facilitates telepathy and your ability to communicate, your self-expression, as well as depth in listening. It has a freer, higher frequency of creativity than the second chakra (not better, just different). This is the creativity of self-expression. Through your fifth-chakra communication, you create and explore your inner identity, your eternal ever-growing self. The energy of the fifth chakra also supports and creatively participates in the inner or psychic creation of events.

The sixth chakra: intellect, beliefs, and clairvoyance

Your sixth chakra is a complex in the center of your head, but, for simplicity's sake, you may envision it as two cones of energy, one facing forward, the other facing backward. The two cones meet at the pituitary gland, located about two inches behind the eyebrows. There are numerous chakras in the head, such as the famous "third eye," located at the center of the eyebrows, and the chakra located at the pineal gland in the center of the head. Later in this book, you will learn to rest your awareness just behind and above the pineal gland and look out through your third eye to see clairvoyantly. Both the pineal gland and the resting place (behind and above the pineal gland) are often called the center of the head. The center of the head, where the light of your soul resides, is a very lovely, calm, and comfortable place to rest and center your awareness.

Emerging from the sixth chakra is your clairvoyance, thinking, ability to visualize, and your belief systems. Through your sixth chakra, you see and create the structured energies we call "pictures." Through visualization, you initiate and direct the inner psychic creation of your reality.

The seventh chakra: wisdom and knowingness

The seventh chakra, also called the crown chakra, is at the top of your head and is frequently seen as a single cone of swirling energy facing upward. This is where the entire cycle of being, with all its gifts, takes place: The gift of creation, the gift of preservation, and the gift of destruction.[2] Through this chakra you can understand a complete cycle of experience in one instant. Hence, the seventh chakra is pure intuition, knowingness. Through your perception of the entire cycle of creation, you create meaning from your experiences.

On a less abstract note, the frequency you run in your crown sets the tone with which you will interact with the world.

Chakra Cleaning

Your developing psychic/emotional awareness will be greatly enhanced by cleaning and removing blockages from your chakras. If performed daily, the following exercise will provide extraordinary benefit to your health, your grounding, and your understanding of your relationship to yourself and others.

The chakra cleaning exercise begins with bringing your awareness into the center of your head, and grounding and owning the room. Beginning with your foot chakras and moving up one chakra at a time, find the frequency of each chakra. Each chakra will be at a higher frequency than the one before. Depending upon which chakra you are working with, bring a ball of Earth or cosmic energy into the chakra and, with an imaginary pair of "psychic hands," gently open the chakra as wide as it will comfortably go and carefully clean it out. Then bring fresh energy in to fill the cleared space and close the chakra down to the suggested percentage (see page 38). Proceed to the next chakra and repeat the process, all the way up to your crown, and finish the exercise by clearing your hand chakras.

----

[2]Lots of people have trouble with the word "destroy." We encourage you to explore the concept of destruction and to allow yourself to be in touch with your appropriately aggressive energy. New life cannot emerge without some portions being destroyed.

Opening and closing the chakras

In some respects "opening and closing chakras" is a misleading phrase, because chakras are multidimensional and, in the three dimensions of space, they can be seen many different ways depending upon which "slice" of the multiple dimensions you focus on. Still, by "intending" to open the chakras, something does happen that can be seen and felt that makes these psychic organs more open and available to you.

Recalling the cone shape of the chakras, imagine the openings to the chakra, the outermost part of each cone, to be round. Then imagine that the chakras have the ability to open and close like a camera lens, or like the iris of an eye. To open a chakra, imagine you have a pair of psychic hands that gently open it as wide as it will comfortably go. No need to force it. Once you open it, imagine yourself gently cleaning the front and back of each chakra, inside and out, all around.

When you've finished clearing each chakra, you can use your intent and your psychic hands to close the fifth and sixth chakras down to 80 percent, and all your other chakras, including those in your hands and feet, down to 35 percent. What do we mean by closing a chakra to 35 percent? Use your imagination to hypothesize what constitutes being 100 percent open, then, with your psychic hands, close the chakra down to 35 percent of that hypothetical 100 percent opening.

We encourage you to become familiar enough with your chakra system that you can sense what percentages are appropriate for you. It's great to open the chakras and it's very powerful to begin to know how and when it is appropriate to close your chakras down. That way you have more awareness and energy resources to focus on your needs and pleasures. For example, a person whose early experience locked their first chakra open to 90 percent would have large amounts of psychic energy focused on survival issues, even when, objectively, they were quite safe. That energy investment in survival could be redirected more pleasurably elsewhere. With experience, you will be able to choose appropriate and effective percentages, according to your own unique circumstances and needs of the moment.

Using Earth or cosmic energy to clean your chakras

You can use either Earth or cosmic energy to clean and replenish any chakra. We find it appropriate to use Earth energy for your foot chakras and your first, second, and third chakras (those below the heart). For your fourth, fifth, sixth, and seventh chakras and the hand chakras (those at heart level and above), we find it useful to bring down golden cosmic energy. Whenever you bring energy up your body, as for your first, second, and third chakras, you utilize the front channels of your body. When you bring energy down into your system, as for your fourth and fifth chakras, you utilize the back channels of your body. Ascending energy flows up the front of your body, while descending energy flows down the back of your body. For the sixth and seventh chakras, just bring the healing cosmic energy straight in from above.

Exercise 8: *Chakra cleaning*

1. Resting your awareness in the center of the head, breathe gently and deeply into your belly as you ground and own the room.
2. Clean and clear each chakra, one at a time, beginning with the feet, proceeding up the body to the crown, and then clearing the hands.
3. With your psychic hands, gently open each chakra.
4. Clean each chakra with either Earth or cosmic energy. For the foot chakras, and the first, second, and third chakras, use fresh Earth energy. For the hand chakras and the fourth through seventh chakras, use golden cosmic energy.
5. Release any old or excess energy from each chakra.
6. When finished clearing and filling each chakra, close each chakra down to the appropriate percentage (80 percent for the fifth and sixth chakras; 35 percent for all others).

7. Cut off your grounding cord and create a new one.
8. Run Earth and cosmic energy.
9. Check to see that you are still grounded and owning the room.
10. When ready, stand up, stretch, and reverse polarities.

To genuinely release old energy your beliefs must change

Since you create your own reality according to your beliefs, even the energy that you are getting rid of has been with you for some purpose. To release your "junk," you must allow your personality (your beliefs) to change. None of these techniques will work unless you use them to transform your beliefs.

Unprocessed experiences become pain

While the overall goal in becoming more psychically aware is to help you become happier and healthier and more engaged in life, it may very well be that, as you enter into this process, emotional or physical pain arises. Experiences that haven't been processed or resolved become pain in the body, and almost everyone's response to pain is to go *out* of the body. Your awareness may actually be outside your body, which is one of the reasons we spend so much time consciously bringing our awareness into the center of the head. If you go out of the body, you temporarily avoid the pain, but you don't clear the issue.

The techniques you are learning here are designed to intentionally bring you more *into* your body. From there, you can clear the pain from your body and start to enjoy your body and your relationships more deeply.

Only you can monitor your own progress. Some pains might be a reason to see a doctor, some might only accompany growth. By paying attention to your own perceptions and gaining experience, you can know which is which. This is just like the rest of your life, where you decide which headaches to ignore, which to treat with aspirin, and which need medical attention.

A student once protested, "Why do I have to clean my chakras every day? It's like cleaning my house: I don't enjoy that." You can think of it this way: if each time you cleaned house, the house became more beautiful and more luxurious, if you found new rooms that you didn't know you had, or if all the rooms became larger, would you enjoy cleaning the house? That's what you're doing when you clean your chakras. You are creating new and beautiful rooms. You are opening and cleaning your closets. You are transforming your house.

Energy Blocks and Pictures: Your Past, Present, and Future

You may recall from the earlier discussion of chakras that you create pictures in the sixth chakra. Bound-up psychic energy blocks, frozen in time, are called "pictures." As you become clairvoyant, you can often see actual images of unprocessed experiences. Every experience is momentarily created as a picture. Ideally, when each experience is over, the experience is processed and resolved unconsciously by the person. When the experience is processed, the memory is stored in psychic memory banks and the energy held in the picture of the experience becomes free and available very rapidly. When the experience isn't fully processed or resolved, however, the energy stays frozen and unavailable. A little bit of you gets locked into the past.[3] A block is formed which disrupts energy flowing through your aura, like cholesterol deposits disrupt the healthy flow of blood in the physical body.

Blowing or destroying pictures

The next several exercises will allow you to free the bound-up energy in your aura. We call this process "blowing" or "destroying" pictures. Blowing pictures is a technique that breaks

---

[3]This can include pictures of wishes for the future. When energy gets stuck in such a picture, a little bit of you is stuck in past wishes for the future.

up the restriction or the mold around your energy and releases the bound creative energy. It is a powerful way to free
yourself of the hold of the past, often called karma.

You may see, feel, or hear pictures in a variety of ways.
They often appear as specks of dust. They can appear as little
cinder blocks, discordant sounds, or playing cards without
images. Occasionally, they appear as snapshots of the event
that caused the block. These snapshots can sometimes even
appear in three dimensions, and sometimes as three dimen-
sional movies, though that is more rare. Each of you will perceive and experience your pictures in a manner unique to
you. Validate your perceptions, however subtle they may be
at first. Your perceptions are growing.

Create a rose for blowing pictures

Because of its deep archetypal symbolism and the healing
"heart" energy associated with it, we use a rose to set the
stage for blowing pictures.[4] In the next exercise, you'll simply
practice creating roses.

Exercise 9: *Creating a rose*

1. From the center of your head, ground and own the
   room, and breathe gently and deeply into your belly.
2. At about eye level and at arm's length in front of you,
   playfully imagine (see, feel, or hear) a rose 4 to 6
   inches in diameter and give it a color.[5]
3. Relax, and imagine the detail and color filling in.
4. When you feel as though you can sense your rose,
   allow it to simply dissolve.
5. Practice creating several roses, letting each dissolve
   when finished.

---

[4]You don't have to use a rose. You could use any neutral metaphor. Some
people enjoy using other flowers. Sometimes people use a desktop.

[5]White is too high a frequency and black is too low a frequency for our
purposes here.

6. When you are comfortable with the process, playfully create another rose and imagine that it has a kind of magnetic ability that can attract and pull pictures out of your aura. Then let it dissolve.
7. Practice creating several such roses, letting each dissolve when you're finished.
8. Release any energy you are ready to release, and run some Earth and cosmic energy.
9. When finished, stand up, stretch, and reverse polarities.

Using your gift of destruction

You may recall that the seventh chakra, your crown chakra, has the gift of destruction. In the next exercise, you will learn how to use your gift of destruction to free the energy bound in your pictures. Once you have attracted a picture onto your rose, send a beam or a ball of golden cosmic energy down from your crown chakra to the picture on the rose and blow it up.[6] Once you destroy your picture, intend that the energy released from that picture recycle back into your crown chakra. From there, without need of your conscious attention, it will naturally flow back to where it belongs.

Destroying pictures is *not* an act of inappropriate aggression. Destroying pictures simply releases the "stuckness" of an experience. It breaks the mold, frees the energy, and brings you into current time.

What happens to an experience when you destroy a picture?

What happens, you may ask, to the experience when you blow up the picture? You keep the experience. Energy need

---

[6]Blowing up a picture means destroying or exploding a picture, not increasing the size of the picture like "blowing up" a picture in the photographic sense.

not be inside a picture floating in your aura for you to keep the experience; the memory is automatically filed as pure memory in the back of your head. Once you've had an experience, you can always bring that experience back, fill it with energy, and recreate it as a picture. We all have memories that are dear to us that we recall from time to time. Yours may be your first love or the birth of a child. You don't need to trap frozen versions of those experiences in your aura to recall the experiences from time to time. When you are through reminiscing, you can explode your picture, freeing your energy while saving the experience for eternity.

Destroying pictures is changing beliefs

Some people believe you have to find and destroy every picture in your aura, but that simply isn't true. Remember, these techniques are just ways to change and heal beliefs. Techniques are just natural bridges, ways for different portions of yourself to communicate. Underneath all technique is your relationship with your Deep Self. Ultimately, since you create your own reality according to your own beliefs, when you clear enough pictures connected with a specific belief, your belief changes. And the remaining pictures will just evaporate, because your Deep Self will take care of them. Your energy actually changes when you blow a picture, but blowing a picture also informs your Deep Self, "This is the direction I'm taking. I want to become freer around this particular issue."

Remember to fill your aura with fresh energy

When you destroy a picture, you remove energy from your aura. Whenever you remove energy from your aura, by releasing old energy or by destroying pictures, you always fill your aura back up with fresh energy. During this next exercise, you probably won't know exactly from where in your aura your pictures come, and that lack of specific knowledge won't matter. Just run some Earth and cosmic energy when you're done blowing pictures, and replenish your whole aura.

Blowing pictures: pleasant and unpleasant events

For your first experience blowing pictures, remember two events, one pleasant and one mildly unpleasant. Just imagine each event as a "picture." We encourage you to leave heavily charged events until you've had some practice with these techniques. Let your intuition help you choose. Work with one picture at a time, beginning with the unpleasant event.

First, ground and own the room, then create a rose in front of you and imagine the picture of your unpleasant event on the rose. Your rose will hold it for you. Next, imagine a beam or a ball, or even a series of balls, of golden cosmic energy streaming down from your crown chakra and blowing up your picture. You can blow up the picture without even touching the rose or you can blow up the rose and picture simultaneously. Whichever way you choose, at the end of the session make sure you explode any roses you created and any pictures they attracted. If you are somewhat clairaudient, you may hear the pictures "pop." If you are more kinesthetic (feeling oriented), you may feel that the picture is dissolved and gone. Those who are more visual (clairvoyant), may be able to simply see that the picture has been destroyed. Use your imagination and have fun. However you make it disappear will be fine.

Repeat the process with your picture of a pleasant event. When you are finished blowing each picture, intend that the newly freed energy from each picture (which is your own energy) be recycled back through your crown, to wherever it belongs. Run some Earth and cosmic energy to be certain the newly cleared space in your aura has been filled.

For the purpose of this initial exercise, you will be destroying a balance of pleasant and unpleasant pictures, one each. Once you are familiar with the process and utilizing the techniques that follow, you may want to spend an entire meditation session exploding all unpleasant or all pleasant pictures, or a spontaneous mix of pleasant and unpleasant pictures.

Exercise 10: *Blowing pleasant and unpleasant pictures*

1. Resting your awareness in the center of your head, breathe gently and deeply into your belly, as you ground and own the room.
2. Imagine a rose in front of you at arm's length and eye level.
3. Let your rose attract and hold your unpleasant picture.
4. Spend a moment observing your picture and how you feel.
5. When ready, explode the rose and unpleasant picture with the golden cosmic energy.
6. Check your grounding and breathe gently into your belly.
7. Create a new rose.
8. Let your rose attract and hold your pleasant picture.
9. Spend a moment observing your picture and how you feel.
10. Explode the rose and pleasant picture with the golden cosmic energy.
11. Recycle your energy from the exploded pictures and roses back through your crown chakra.
12. Check your grounding, breathe gently and deeply, and say hello to your body.
13. When ready, stand up, stretch, and reverse polarities.

Lighting up other pictures

When you focus on a picture or a belief, you "light up" other pictures, pictures involving the same issues or emotions. Just as seeing a happy movie can remind you of happy events in your own life, paying attention to your experiences tends to trigger memories of other experiences. Clairvoyantly, the parallel pictures suddenly shine, that is, they stand out from the background of energy. They "light up."

In the future, when you blow up a picture, you will probably want to destroy all the pictures that the first picture lights up, that is, any pictures that rise to your attention. You may not see them, you may just "feel" or "know" that other pictures have been lit up. You can explode them on a rose, one at a time or in groups. You may find a group of pictures clustered together. Sometimes there may be too many to explode easily in one blast. If this happens, you can imagine the pictures are like sheets of newspaper burning in a fire, just curling up one page at a time.

Occasionally, you may find a picture that you'll need to blow up repeatedly, perhaps every day for a month. If this happens, add a little amusement. Approach the picture with a sense of adventure and keep exploding it. It is also very useful to know how and when to "set aside" a highly charged picture or issue for a while.

Consciously setting an issue aside

If, while meditating, you have a very highly charged and painful memory arise, you can literally "set it aside." Giving yourself permission to set it aside creates space around the issue and gives you time to build your readiness to deal with it. Say hello to it, and realize that you don't have to clear the whole issue at once. You may just put a curtain around it and come back to it later when you're feeling more ready.

It's fun and empowering to create your own metaphor for setting aside an issue. You can place it in a closet and open the door when you're ready. Or you can place it in a chest and unlock it when you're ready to bring it out. Setting aside an issue, while affirming that you will deal with the issue when you are ready, validates your process and helps you realize that you have a right to say, "I'm going to take this a little bit at a time." You can allow your unconscious mind to work on the issue at its own pace and bring it to your conscious attention from time to time as you are ready. You can consciously check on the issue when you have the time and the energy, deciding how much of the issue you wish to work on at any one time.

Highly charged issues are rarely resolved in one session. Setting something aside acknowledges the truth that you're always going to have issues to work on, that you will never be "done" with all your issues. It would be denial, of course, to lock something away with the intent of never returning. But the intent here is to return to the issue as soon as you can, and to be resourceful in dealing with it.

Other people's pictures in our space

We often program each other by throwing pictures into each other's space. Sometimes you'll find pictures that aren't yours. You can't easily blow up someone else's pictures, but you can send them back. If a picture doesn't blow up after several tries, ask yourself, "Is this my picture or someone else's?" If it is someone else's picture, send it back, preferably with amusement. You don't necessarily need to know whose picture it is. If you don't know, you can drop it all the way down your grounding cord and just intend that it "return to sender."

Suggestions for Further Explorations

1. Become aware of the profound effect that emotions and events have on your chakras.
2. Pay particular attention to your second-chakra. Practice opening or closing it, and then notice how it is an hour later. Remember, second-chakra energy is good, but if you keep the second chakra wide open all the time, it can be problematic. You could be letting other people's energy into your aura, creating a more difficult time owning your space.
3. With some amusement, bring any pictures back that you may have unconsciously thrown into the auras of your co-workers, friends, and loved ones. Then, explode your pictures and recycle your energy.

Chapter Three

The Third Relationship:
With Others

We now move into the third relationship, your relationship to others (everyone from your pets to your guides). We are all interconnected. That interconnectedness is one of the greatest joys in being human. These relationships can get stuck, however, and that is what we will explore next.

Distinguishing Your Own Energy from Other People's Energy

While it is true that we are all one, humanity's current exploration in physical reality is based on free will and individuation. The way in which the Supreme Being has set up this intricate dance of life on planet Earth, the way in which you are able to experience your free will, is through your unique energy. Your essence energy is marked as yours, whether it is in your aura or someone else's.

A major part of your intuitive and emotional growth is learning how to recognize just what is your energy and what isn't your energy. Learning how to distinguish whose energy is in your space can be a very effective tool for owning your body and aura.

Relationships are a collaboration. Once you recognize another's energy in your space, you can send it back to them. That is, however, only half of the equation. Perhaps, even more important, when you find someone's energy is in your space, you'll always find your energy in their space too. So, in addition to sending their energy back, you must take responsibility for your own energy and pull it out of their space. You may want to take a little time to blow the pictures around the issues and beliefs that are involved. Whether the particular issues or beliefs involved are obvious isn't always important. You can just create a rose and intend that it attract the pictures that allowed energy to enter your aura. Then you can explode the rose with the pictures.

If thirty-five lifetimes ago, you had a relationship with someone and you didn't complete your karma with him or her, you may still have some of their energy in your space and they may still have some of your energy in their space. You will find energy in your aura from your parents, your family, your friends, your boss, your ex-lovers, your children, people who have passed on, your past lives, your guides, people you've never met in this life, and even your cats and dogs. This statement may seem overwhelming at first, but you can relax. It has been part of the natural anatomy of relationships on our planet for a very long time.

You can't entirely clear your energy from others, but you can relax and use your new understanding and skills to improve, not perfect, the framework of your relationships, a little at a time.

Energy which is not yours contains wishes, tendencies, and opinions which are not those of your soul. If someone else's energy is in your space, it clouds your judgment. For example, when you find an uncontrollable emotion, it has large components of someone else's energy. Emotions composed of your own energy may be unpleasant, but you will always have resources to use them appropriately. If your energy is in someone else's aura, it not only retards their growth, it is unavailable to you. As you sort your energy out, the effect will be astonishing, the benefit immeasurable.[1]

---

[1]In this system, we do run neutral energy such as Earth and cosmic energy to support our body's and personality's connection with the soul. The exact interaction of our energy with neutral energies is beyond the scope of this book. One could say, however, that even neutral energies are used only to help us connect with and utilize our own energy.

The vacuum-cleaner rose

To your growing collection of energy tools, you'll now add a vacuum-cleaner rose, a tool designed to help you distinguish and sort out your energy from others. You will likely find this versatile tool invaluable, as it provides a method by which you can easily pull other people's energies out of your aura, and a method to return that energy to its original owner.

Your vacuum-cleaner rose complements, but doesn't replace, your picture-blowing rose. Remember, your picture-blowing rose works specifically with your personal energy, attracting your own pictures out of your aura, which you then explode and recycle back through your crown. The vacuum-cleaner rose works specifically with other people's energy, pulling other people's energy out of your space and sending the energy down its grounding cord to Earth's center. Earth then recycles that energy back to its original owner.

To create a vacuum-cleaner rose, ground and own the room. Then imagine a rose out in front of you which has the ability to "vacuum" out and hold other people's energy. Imagine the rose has its own grounding cord. Say to yourself, "My vacuum-cleaner rose now has a grounding cord." And, poof, it's done, effortlessly. Then just allow other people's energy to flow down the cord to Mother Earth, where she'll gladly recycle it back to its original owner for you.

Exercise 11: *Creating a vacuum cleaner rose*

1. Resting your awareness in the center of your head, breathe gently and deeply into your belly as you ground and own the room.
2. At about eye level and at arm's length in front of you, imagine (see, feel, or hear) a rose 4 to 6 inches in diameter.
3. Playfully give it the ability to vacuum other people's energy out of your aura.
4. Give it its own grounding cord, which will allow other people's energy to flow down to Earth's center and be recycled.

5. When comfortable with your creation, explode the rose and recycle your energy back into your crown.
6. Practice creating and destroying several such roses.
7. When finished, stand up, stretch, and reverse polarities.

Distinguishing your father's energy from your own

In the following exercise, you'll distinguish and compare your energy to another's. We find that working with your father's energy is a great place to start. Even if, in this lifetime, you've never met your biological father, you'll still find some of his energy in your aura. If you have a stepfather, or a very important male who has acted as a father to you, you may choose to work with his energy instead.

We're not picking on fathers. Your father's energy is not necessarily bad; it is just not *your* energy. Remember: to engage life more deeply and authentically, you have to run your own unique energy. No one else's energy works as well for you as your own.

John: I'll never forget the first reading I ever did. I was reading a man in his mid-sixties and saw this really beautiful energy in his space, which was his mother's energy. It was very sweet, very lovingly intended, yet I could see quite clearly that it had been constraining him his entire life. It wasn't his version of who he was; it was her version of who he should be.

No one has to accept energy back

Sometimes your father, or any entity with whom you might be working, won't want their energy back. That's okay; no one has to accept his or her energy back. You can give the energy to a guide. You can give it to Earth. You can give it to the Sun. You can give it to the Supreme Being. You're not deciding what's appropriate for other people; you're simply deciding and acting upon what you choose to retain in your aura.

Exercise 12: *Recognizing two*
energies as different from one another

1. Rest your awareness in the center of your head, breathe gently and deeply into your belly, as you ground and own the room.
2. Create a vacuum-cleaner rose with a grounding cord, out in front of you.
3. Let it vacuum some of your father's energy out of your aura, and hold it for you to observe.
4. Move your father's rose 12 inches to your left.
5. Create another vacuum-cleaner rose.
6. Allow it to draw some of your own energy onto it.
7. Move your rose 12 inches to your right.
8. Remember to breathe gently and deeply into your belly and compare the similarities and differences.
9. Acknowledge your emotions and give them space. You may, if you choose, stop and blow any pictures which light up.
10. When ready, destroy your father's rose, letting Earth recycle his energy back to him.
11. Destroy your rose and recycle your energy back into your crown.
12. Check to see that you are still grounded and owning the room.
13. Release any energy you are ready to release.
14. Fill your aura with fresh Earth and cosmic energy.
15. When ready, stand up, stretch, and reverse polarities.

Begin to recognize the different influences in your aura

It's likely that your father will never consciously perceive your sending his energy back to him, though he may may do so unconsciously. The point isn't to change him, or anyone, but to begin to recognize the different influences you hold in your space, so that you can take appropriate responsibility. After you have moved a ton or so of your father's energy out of your space, there will still be other tons remaining. As we said earlier, you may regard this clearing as a miraculous kind of house cleaning, which makes your house bigger, more beautiful, more appropriate for your self. The clearing becomes a lot of fun.

Some people who have great relationships with their fathers report that they are reluctant to send their father's energy back. Remember: you aren't eliminating your ability to experience your father's energy. It's just far more effective for you to run your own energy, your own opinions, your own desires and wishes for yourself. As you own your own space more and more, you'll have an increased capacity to relate to your father on a deeper level—a more direct soul-to-soul level. This will also improve your relationship at a personal level.

Headaches or tiredness after removing energy

Following this exercise, some people have reported that, as they moved their father's energy out, they either got a headache or a headache went away, or they became very tired. These experiences are common, though everyone's experience differs.

Often parents jump into their children's space to try to "train" them how to think, or be, or feel, or act. If a headache clears up, you can take that as a sign that you are effectively beginning to clear out some of your parent's energy. If you get very tired or get a headache while doing this exercise, you may be running into unconscious resistance to your moving their energy out, or you may even be experiencing your *own* resistance to letting go of their influence.

This is when your amusement and your sense of adventure come to your rescue. Grounding, owning the room, running energy, and blowing pictures all help you avoid discomforts. You can even place a little grounding cord into a headache and allow it to drain away the discomfort. Grounding techniques work well for a variety of body pains.

When you meditate, pictures light up and energy blockages that were always present can begin to ache, much like when you begin to exercise after long inactivity. Just as with proper exercise, proper meditation will raise your overall health, making you feel better. For every ache "caused" by meditation, a hundred aches are ended or avoided. Pain sometimes occurs when new flowing energy meets old resistance. Bringing that resistance to your attention leads to information well worth exploring.

To help you find some amusement, think of someone dear to you. Take a moment to consider whether you may have unconsciously jumped into their space on occasion—perhaps with the best of intentions, to help them understand, or be, or feel, or act in a certain way. Is it possible that you have crossed someone's boundaries? Many people are surprised when they look closely at their relationships and realize how much of their energy is in other people's auras. With a little practice, you will become more conscious of how your energy behaves.

Your amusement and your sense of adventure become important allies as you become more energy-aware. Life is meant to be an exploration. If you already knew everything, there'd be nothing to explore. No matter how enlightened you are, this world is big enough to continue to challenge you. You will continue to grow. The object isn't to get it all correct; the object is to playfully explore your life.

Being clear

Many systems advocate shielding yourself, using white light or some manner of "protection" to block others' energy from entering your space. That might be necessary on occasion, but is not recommended as a regular practice. There is a critical difference between shielding yourself and being clear. We encourage being clear. No energy can stick in your space without your cooperation, usually an unconscious collaboration. There is always an aspect of you that invites any energy, good, bad, or indifferent, into your space. Addressing that aspect of yourself is crucial to your individuation, to engaging your life.

As you become clearer and begin to own your identity, you may discover you need shielding only rarely. As you become more capable in threatening situations, recognizing your right to feel safe and more established in your identity, your clarity will protect you.

Comprehensive Chakra Cleaning

The next exercise combines all the techniques discussed so far in a comprehensive chakra cleaning. You will ground, own the room, run energy, open the chakras, clean the chakras, blow pictures, release energy which isn't yours, reclaim your own energy, close chakras to appropriate settings, and fill the aura with fresh Earth and cosmic energy. Following the completion of this exercise, your aura will be unmistakably clearer and your energy will be running much more smoothly throughout your aura. We will walk you through each step, and then you can use the outline to go through the exercise at your leisure.

Chakra cleaning

While breathing gently into your abdomen, bring your awareness into the center of your head, ground and own the room, and, one at a time, find the frequency of each chakra, beginning with your foot chakras and moving upward. Depending upon which chakra you are working with, bring a ball of Earth or cosmic energy into it and, with the aid of your imaginary psychic hands, gently open the chakra, front and back, as wide as it will comfortably open. With care and nurturing, clean each chakra. Be gentle and playful with yourself. Imagine using an etheric whiskbroom, or a silky-soft chamois cloth, or, another favorite, a pliable etheric hose with an adjustable stream of Earth or cosmic energy that can help you clear and soothe any hard-to-reach spaces.

After you clear the chakra, create a pair of picture-blowing roses, one for the forward-facing part of the chakra you are working on, and one for the backward-facing part. Blow the pictures, front and back, that light up. Then destroy the roses, remembering to recycle your energy back through your crown. Create a pair of vacuum-cleaner roses, one for the front of the chakra, one for the back, and vacuum out other people's opinions or energies that you are ready to release. Destroy those roses. Let Earth recycle other people's energy for you. Then blow up your vacuum-cleaner rose, and recycle the energy you utilized to create it back into your own crown. Bring fresh Earth or cosmic energy in to fill all the freshly cleared space. Thank your chakra for being so willing to change, then close it down, front and back, to the suggested percentage and proceed to the next chakra and repeat the process.

When finished, retrieve all of the energy you've put in other people's auras by breathing all your energy back, or by using the rose-satellite-dish technique (see below). Then, in celebration of all the shifts you have made, congratulate yourself and create a new grounding cord for the emerging you.

Reclaiming your energy with a satellite-dish rose

In the beginning of the book you were introduced to an easy breathing technique for retrieving your energy from other times and other spaces—inhaling your energy back into current time from where it had been trapped. Another versatile tool for reclaiming large amounts of energy is a *satellite-dish rose*. It's fun and simple to use. Just imagine a big satellite-dish rose above your head and direct it to any time or place you'd like to clear. Then allow it to pull your energy back into your crown and back into current time. You can reclaim your energy from this lifetime, as well as from your past lives. When finished, blow up the rose and remember to recycle its energy back through your crown.

Creating and destroying roses

Exploding lots of pictures at once is called blowing roses or creating and destroying roses. It's helpful to realize that you won't be able to "see" the content of the individual pictures, because you'll be pulling them out so quickly. You might release a thousand pictures in five minutes. You won't have time, and there is simply no need to linger over each one of them. You're letting go of pictures that you are ready to release, so you can just let them flow. Be assured that specific beliefs, events, or issues that need your individual attention will reveal themselves as you are ready to work on them. If a particular picture does come individually to your attention while doing this exercise, you can decide whether or not to stop and spend time with it.

It is easy to neglect your back while doing these exercises. Exploding roses in front and behind will help you remember to clear your whole aura.

Exercise 13: *Comprehensive chakra cleaning*

1. Resting your awareness in the center of your head, breathe gently and deeply into your belly, as you ground and own the room.
2. Beginning with your feet and moving up one chakra at a time, gently open each chakra, front and back, with your psychic hands.
3. Clean each chakra with Earth or cosmic energy. For your foot chakras and the first, second, and third chakras, use fresh Earth energy. For your hand chakras and the fourth through seventh chakras use golden cosmic energy.
4. Create and destroy roses for any pictures that light up, front and back.
5. Recycle your energy back into your crown.
6. Create a pair of vacuum-cleaner roses for each chakra, front and back, and vacuum out other people's energy.
7. Destroy your vacuum-cleaner roses when finished, recycling your energy.
8. Fill each chakra with the appropriate Earth or cosmic energy.
9. Close each chakra down to an appropriate percentage for you, for example, 80 percent for the fifth and sixth chakras, 60 percent for the third, fourth, and seventh chakras, 40 percent for the foot and hand chakras, and 30 percent for the first and second chakras.
10. Reclaim your own energy from other people's auras.

11. Create a new grounding cord and own the room.
12. Release any excess energy.
13. Congratulate yourself and thank your body for being so willing to change.
14. When ready, stand up, stretch, and reverse polarities.

Cords

A cord establishes an ongoing psychic relationship, a continuous exchange of energy, between people. Clairvoyantly, cords often appear similar to an umbilical cord between people, usually from one chakra to another, though cords may be found throughout the aura and the body. Usually, with some important exceptions, the only cord that supports growth is your grounding cord. Most cords, even if sent unconsciously, seek to control or influence another in some manner. It is through cords that we program each other and, no matter how well intended, cords limit personal growth. In this system, we remove cords when we find them. When cords light up for you, you can assume that you are ready to address the need or belief and begin releasing it.

John and Gloria: We're not removing all our cords, just the ones that light up, that is, that come to our attention. We believe that any time we see a cord in our own space, we are ready to start releasing it. That belief doesn't necessarily apply when we see a cord in a client or a student's space. Since he or she may not have seen or felt it yet, he or she may not be ready to address it. If it appears that releasing such a cord could be premature, we might straighten or repair it, or simply note it, then discuss the underlying issue.

Parents and cords

If you are a mother or father of a young child, it is appropriate for you to have some cords with them to help support their learning. Even so, we suggest that you examine your cords with your children. Make sure you are only offering the appropriate energies for each phase in their lives. Stay in current time with their needs. Eventually, their need will be for you to release them.

When caring for the elderly, cords can be a means of nurturing and support. Even so, you will also want to frequently monitor these cords' appropriateness and be mindful of the elderly person's conscious and unconscious wishes.

Removing cords is a great way to respect and set boundaries

Cords have always been an invisible component in relating. Everyone has cords. Everyone sends cords. Everyone receives cords. As you explore your aura, you may be surprised at how many cords you find. By removing your cords, you'll be able to relate more deeply and authentically than ever before. Removing cords is a great way to respect and set boundaries.

Gloria: When John and I began working together on this book, I was still new to some of the techniques and concepts. One day, he explained how sometimes, when he'd find a cord from someone in his space, he'd gently shake the cord to light it up a little more so that he could clear the underlying issues before he released it. Hearing that solved a mystery for me and explained the puzzling "tugging" sensation I'd had in my throat chakra whenever we finished working together. I realized that, to understand him better while we were working, I had been unconsciously sending cords to his fifth and sixth chakras.

As you learn how to follow your own energy and take responsibility for it, you will send fewer cords and be less likely to invite them into your space. Paradoxically, as you create more separation, you create more space for love. In our opinion, being an autonomous human being is a prerequisite for genuine love. You can only be genuinely interdependent when you are reasonably independent. One objective, as a developing psychic, is to clear a space for love.

Advanced student: Seventeen-year-olds can be quite incommunicative and angry; and living with one as a single parent in a small house was at times excruciatingly painful for both of us. To help the situation, John suggested that I move some of my energy from my son's space twice a day. After just one day, my son began talking to me in complete sentences and did not even get angry when I asked him to repeat himself (because of "rapid speak")! We were actually communicating again. It was at that point that I knew and understood that these techniques really work in our three-dimensional world.

How to remove cords

No cord can exist or continue without at least some unconscious acceptance and collaboration by both parties. To remove the cords that you are ready to release, see, feel, hear, or imagine your psychic hands playfully and gently pulling out, or brushing away, any cords. Go inside, outside, all around each chakra, spherically. Avoid ripping out cords, because, if done from a sense of invalidation, that can leave holes in an aura. Remember your amusement. Gently pull the cords out while blowing the pictures that allowed them into your space.

Sometimes it is enough just to push the cords away; they just vanish. Often, after being pushed away, cords sort of hang around, as if they were waiting to see if you meant it. Blow the pictures that those cords light up. Very often, you'll need to nurture that part of your aura and have a conversation with that part of yourself so you don't let the cords back in. You don't need to know who the cords came from, though very often you will. Table 2 (see page 61) may help you understand the cords often associated with specific chakras.

Can a cord return? Yes, sometimes. If you haven't finished with an issue, it can come back. That's why it's important to blow the pictures around your issues.

Student: When removing cords from my fifth chakra, all kinds of pictures and rules began to light up regarding the proper way to express myself. I then understood why I'd had such a hard time finding my own voice.

Often, you'll uncover another cord related to a new level of the same issue. Each time you remove a cord, the issue heals a little more. Again, you create your own reality according to your beliefs. Removing cords is really addressing your beliefs.

You can assume that you have a cord if, after you send someone's energy back, it returns in a few minutes. Another clue is pain. It is very effective to blow pictures and remove cords and other people's energy from places of pain.

Exercise 14: *Removing cords*

1. Resting your awareness in the center of your head, breathe gently and deeply into your belly, as you ground and own the room.
2. At each chakra, beginning with your feet, moving up to your crown, and ending with your hands, imagine your psychic hands gently removing cords, front, back, all around.
3. Create roses, front and back, and explode pictures, recycling your energy back through your crown.
4. Create vacuum-cleaner roses, front and back, and remove energy. Destroy those roses, letting Mother Earth recycle other people's energy, and recycle your own energy back into your crown.
5. Fill each chakra with the appropriate Earth or cosmic energy.
6. Cut off your old grounding cord and create a new one, then own the room.
7. Release any energy your body or aura is ready to release.
8. Replenish your body and aura.
9. Thank your body for being so willing to change.
10. When ready, stand up, stretch, and reverse polarities.

Asking cords to light up

You can make up your own program using these techniques. For instance, you can ask any cords related to a certain belief or a particular person to light up. Then you can set a comfortable pace for yourself and playfully work with the cords. You can do this for a single session or over time, for a week or two, perhaps longer.

The glass ball technique

A fun and effective technique to help you find cords is to create a glass ball around a chakra and let it light up any cords there. Giving the glass ball different colors will light up different cords. When you're finished, move the glass ball out of your aura and blow it up. Recycle the energy you used to create the glass ball back through your crown.

Gloria: I like to use a glass ball when I'm working with someone with whom I am enmeshed. Before I begin separating our energies, I surround myself with a glass ball (about ten feet in diameter) outside my aura. While removing cords and energy I "listen" to the surface of the ball and I hear the cords that are trying to come back "tinging" or tapping on the glass. This allows me to validate and say hello to their concerns, while I continue to separate our energy. Afterward, I destroy the glass ball and recycle my energy.[2]

Contracts

Most cords represent simple agreements with others. As you continue to work with cords, you'll begin to perceive a specific kind of cord called a *contract*. A contract is an agreement between two people made at a very deep level, a unity level. They can be hard to remove. Contracts can be from this or other lifetimes. If you find a cord that doesn't budge, even

---

[2]Though this approach requires some clairaudient ability, you might find it fun to explore seeing, feeling, or hearing the cords.

after working with it for a while, it is often a contract. If you are advanced, you might raise your energy to a unity level and remove the cord from that level. But, even as a beginner, you can take heart. If you find such a cord and feel you are ready to release it, remember your amusement. Blow pictures and breathe your energy out of the cord. Explore the beliefs associated with it. Do that for a day, for a week, for a month, and eventually the contract will dissolve. How do you know what beliefs are associated with it? Look at it. Feel it. Listen to it. Ask it. Eventually the beliefs will reveal themselves.

To reiterate: energy in your space is a collaboration

Remember, we believe it is impossible for someone's energy or influence to be in your space without your energy matching or giving permission to it in some manner, based upon some belief of yours. The collaboration can be from this lifetime, or from past lives. Certain energies in your space can present problems. They can give you headaches, and can even make you quite ill. That's a part of life, like traffic jams are a part of life.[3] As you know, you can honk and scream and make a nuisance of yourself, but it just doesn't help the situation.

We suggest that you keep your amusement and pace yourself. Work with other people's energy for as long it takes to move the energy out and, more importantly, explore your beliefs regarding the relationship.

There's an important refinement in understanding the concept of "energy in your space": it helps to understand that working with "my energy" versus "their energy" is just a belief system.

Double negation

This refinement can be understood by a double negation process. The first negation ("It's not my energy") recognizes and negates the idea that another's energy is you. However, if

---

[3] Traffic jams are a perfect opportunity to blow "impatience" pictures.

you stop at that recognition, you can become alienated and fearful about other people's energy. You must to take the next, very sophisticated, step.

The second more subtle negation that has to take place is negating the *negation* about the energy being you: "The energy isn't me, but in a subtle way it *is*." It is you, because it is functioning within your system as sanctioned by you. Some mirror belief invited it in. And if you send it out without recognizing that you are changing or transforming *yourself*, you can end up negating your own need to change. That misses the point and can be quite unfortunate. Your whole purpose is to send the energy back with the recognition that, in the sending, you are intending to change yourself.

This system's greatest weakness

Every system has weaknesses. This system's greatest weakness is that, if you fail to realize, or if you forget, that you consciously and unconsciously create your own reality, IT IS VERY EASY TO SLIP INTO OBJECTIFICATION AND VICTIMIZATION. If you are unable to remove someone's energy from your space, if you objectify your problem as "somebody else being in your space" and act as if they are the cause of your problem, you can fall into a feeling of victimization. That is this system's greatest weakness.

It is essential to understand that you are not a victim, that you are responsible for your own feelings, thoughts, and responses to others. It may be that you have to avoid someone who causes you pain. But eventually you will have to deal with the underlying beliefs, and in that sense you are not a victim (you may be objectively wronged, but ultimately the responsibility for, and power in, your life is yours). Because of the terminology, this system can subtly bias people toward objectifying and feeling victimized, unless they are very scrupulous. You must keep reminding yourself: "I create my own reality."

The only way this system will truly work well for you is from a state of neutrality, forgiveness, exploration, playfulness, amusement, interest, and acceptance.

Recognizing underlying mirror beliefs

You can begin to identify your mirror beliefs, or needs that allow energy or cords into your space, by asking the energy to reveal those beliefs to you. Some beliefs will be apparent, others may surprise you. When you find an energy in your space, place it out on a rose in front of you, and observe it for a while. Notice its characteristics. Then ask the energy, or ask yourself, what purpose does it serve in your space? What is it meant to teach you? What does your soul want you to learn from it? What is your partner mirroring in you?

If the energy feels controlling, ask yourself if perhaps you've given your power away to someone, or if you are controlling others in some way. For example, in a marriage, one partner may openly and emotionally make demands, while the other is coolly, "intellectually objective," which can be a covert way of controlling others. Both partners may be engaged in a kind of attempt to control. Each may be mirroring the other. In another example, if someone's energy in your space feels angry, you may perhaps have some forgiveness work to do. Your reasons for allowing the cord or energy into your space will be utterly unique for you.

Once you begin to genuinely recognize a belief that limits you—when you can see it, hear it, feel it, or know it—it is on its way out. The most difficult part is over. It may take longer than you want it to, but once you've perceived the energy, you are over half-way there in your ability to release it. You can use the techniques in this system or others, such as Neuro Linguistic Programming (NLP), to change the beliefs.

Common Messages of Corded Chakras

Table 2 (see page 61) describes some common messages of cords associated with certain chakras. This table, far from being definitive, is meant to be a starting point. You will find cords abide by few rules and can be found anywhere throughout the aura and the body, including in the organs.

Table 2. Common Messages of Corded Chakras

Chakra	Common Messages	Affirmations
First Chakra	I will save you Save me Ground me I will ground you	I can ground myself I am very capable I am safe I live in a safe universe I nurture and own my first chakra
Second Chakra	Feel my emotions I feel your emotions Own my body I own your body	My appropriate boundaries My feelings I nurture and own my second chakra
Third Chakra	Tell me what to do I will control your energy Take my power Give me power	I know my own will I am empowered I can take my time to understand others I nurture and own my third chakra
Fourth Chakra	I love you Love me Complete me I will complete you	I know my own heart I am loved I love myself I nurture and own my heart chakra
Fifth Chakra	Let me speak for you Speak for me I hear you Hear me I will say what you want to hear Say what I want to hear	I speak for myself I listen openly, deeply and playfully I speak clearly I nurture and own my fifth chakra
Sixth Chakra	I see you Pay attention to me What do you see See what I want you to see See for me Let me see it for you	I can see for myself I can let myself be seen I can try to see another's viewpoint I nurture and own my sixth chakra
Seventh Chakra	Let me think for you Think for me I own you Own me	I know I have my own certainty I nurture and own my crown chakra

Suggestions for Further Explorations

1. Repeat Exercise 12, Recognizing two different energies (see page 47), with different significant people in your life. Recall your energy from their space and lovingly send their energy back to them.
2. While grounding and owning the room, practice putting a grounding cord on any headaches or minor pains.
3. Clean all of your chakras at least once a week if you can. You can make it easier on yourself by cleaning one chakra a day.
4. Give your family a gift by playfully removing any unnecessary cords you have with them. Contemplate the beliefs that helped create and sustain those cords.

Chapter Four

The Fourth Relationship: Your God of the Heart

We are all multidimensional beings. Portions of us are active in other dimensions, right now and all the time. Some of those portions are vast beyond understanding, and still, in some sense, they are us, the very ground out of which we grow. Our knowing this, even if we do not consciously interact with those portions, helps them to aid us unconsciously. Most portions of ourselves in other dimensions are beyond the scope of this book. There is one vast multidimensional portion of ourselves, however, a central aspect of ourselves, which is readily available as a resource in our daily lives. We call it the "God of the Heart." It is the portion of God that looks out toward the individual, and the portion of the individual that looks in toward God. This portion, known also as the Deep Self or Higher Self, underlies all experience, supporting, loving, and enthusiastically embracing each aspect of our lives. The God of the Heart collaborates from a deeper dimension with each of our physical selves.

The following four God-of-the-Heart exercises will help refine your ability to consciously communicate with your God of the Heart. The first exercise will familiarize you with the glorious God-of-the-Heart energy. The second opens a conscious dialog between you and your essence. The third requires a partner and enables you to receive a message from your partner's God of the Heart, which you then convey to them. The fourth introduces a simple, powerful method of collaborating with your God of the Heart to help you work through specific issues with other people.

Saying hello to your God of the Heart

To get in touch with your God of the Heart, imagine moving up your chakras like a ladder. Begin by simply seeing, feeling, hearing, or imagining your first-chakra energy, then your second-chakra energy, then your third-chakra energy, all the way up to your crown-chakra energy. This part of the exercise should take 10 to 30 seconds per chakra.

Once you've reached your crown chakra, take another step and move your attention to a spot a foot above and a foot in front of your crown chakra. There, hypothesize that you can see, hear, or feel a pinpoint of the most brilliant, diamond-white or clear light that you can imagine. Say hello to your God of the Heart, and allow it to greet you.

Bring your God of the Heart back over your head, down your back, and into your heart chakra. Then (just for this first exercise) take some time to familiarize yourself with your essence energy by expanding the clear light until it fills your entire body and aura. Rest in your God of the Heart's infinitely playful, infinitely compassionate, infinitely courageous, infinitely adventurous, infinitely loving embrace. This completely supportive energy underlies all of your experience.

Next, condense the light back down to a diamond pinpoint, move it back until it rests about 4 to 8 inches behind your body, and allow it to remain there. You can pretend that you are parking it in the fifth or sixth dimension and that may help to remind you that its frequency is too high for you, as a human, to hold and still be effectively grounded and present in daily life. Working with the high frequency of each God-of-the-Heart exercise will require you to pay special attention to your grounding.

Exercise 15: *Saying hello to your God of the Heart*

1. Resting your awareness in the center of your head, breathe gently and deeply into your belly as you ground and own the room.

2. Create and destroy roses.
3. Find the frequency of each chakra, beginning with your first and moving to your crown.
4. Move your attention one foot above and one foot in front of your crown.
5. Imagine the most brilliant, clear, diamond-white light, your God of the Heart, greeting you. Say hello in return.
6. Bring that clear diamond-white light behind you and into your heart chakra.
7. Experience that infinite light and love expanding throughout your entire body and aura. Spend some time being nurtured and supported by that light.
8. Allow the brilliant light to condense to a pinpoint in the center of your chest.
9. Ask the light to move to a place 4 to 8 inches behind your body.
10. Run Earth and cosmic energy.
11. Make certain that you are grounded and in your body.
12. When ready, slowly stand up, stretch, and reverse polarities.

Your God of the Heart's rose

In the next exercise, a rose becomes a special meeting place for you and your God of the Heart to communicate with each other. To create your special meeting place, simply imagine a beautiful rose at eye level, out in front of you. Invite your God of the Heart onto the rose and, remembering your amusement, talk about anything you'd like. We recommend that you keep it simple. You might begin by asking easy questions, or by sharing whatever thoughts you would like to share. Sometimes, people find it helpful to stay with one subject per session. Play. When finished, ask your God of the Heart to move back behind you again, destroy the rose, and recycle your energy back through your crown.

Exercise 16: *Your God of the Heart's rose*

1. Resting your awareness in the center of your head, breathe gently and deeply into your belly, as you ground and own the room.
2. Create and destroy roses.
3. Find the frequency of each chakra, beginning with your first and moving to your crown.
4. Move your attention one foot above and one foot in front of your crown.
5. Imagine your God of the Heart greeting you.
6. Say hello and invite your God of the Heart onto the rose.
7. Ask your questions, and see, feel or hear the answers.
8. When finished, thank your God of the Heart and ask it to move 4 to 8 inches behind your body, at heart level.
9. Run some Earth and cosmic energy.
10. Make certain that you are well grounded and in your body.
11. When ready, slowly stand up, stretch, and reverse polarities.

The God-of-the-Heart reading

The God-of-the-Heart reading is a psychic reading you do for someone else. In this delightful exercise, you communicate with a friend's God of the Heart and convey what you learn to them. Then you can exchange roles and have them do the same for you.

Certainty

When giving a psychic reading, we suggest that you cultivate an unusual kind of certainty. Avoid certainty that you're "right" or certainty that you "know" what the other person should do. Only be certain that you have sensations and perceptions, not that your sensations or perceptions are right.

Be willing to share your perceptions (or what you think you perceive) and your interpretations. That's the limit of your responsibility. If you stay in that particular style of certainty, you will avoid imposing your view on the other person.

Strangely enough, it doesn't matter whether your information is right or not—it's the other person's responsibility to decide whether the information is useful to them. And, if it doesn't seem useful for them, that's okay, too. You've fulfilled your responsibility by sharing your perceptions.

Information can come to you in various forms. Some information will require interpretation, some will not.[1] For example, your friend's God of the Heart may say, "Take that job." While your friend still has to decide whether or not to take the job, you probably know what their God of the Heart meant. If their essence merely shows you a picture of them taking the job, and if it looks or feels good, that too may not need much interpretation. Often, however, communication is symbolic or metaphoric and may require interpretation. An important step in interpreting a communication from the God of the Heart is to discover whose symbol or metaphor is being communicated, your friend's or your own.

Ask for clarification

A surprisingly simple and powerful technique for clarifying information is to ask yourself or your friend's God of the Heart, "What does this mean?" Most people are unsure of their perceptions in the beginning, so just ask for more information and share what you get. For example, you might ask,

---

[1]We're using interpretation in a colloquial sense here, in an everyday sense. If the God of the Heart says, "Take a job with IBM," that statement probably doesn't require a significant amount of interpretation. Ultimately, however, all perception and communication involve some interpretation. If a job is available and being considered with IBM, then little interpretation is necessary. If not, then IBM would be an image to be interpreted according to your own, or the other person's, unique associations.

"Is this my friend's symbol or my symbol?" If it's your symbol, then you can say to yourself, "Okay, what does this symbol mean to me?" If you get an image that you can't understand, you can say, "Okay, God of my partner's heart, I can't make heads or tails of this, can you elaborate?" You can ask yourself, your God of the Heart, the other person's God of the Heart, or even the perception or symbol itself. Doing a reading can be difficult if you think the reading has to come out like a printed page. Doing a reading is really easy if you stay in a resourceful frame of mind. Be willing to share the information, even if you can't specify its meaning or vouch for its accuracy.

Sometimes, information may seem so simple that it takes a certain amount of courage to share it. Often, what you might imagine as ordinary or trite may set up your next communication, or it may communicate something profound.

Student: The message my friend got for me was, "Life is joy," which may seem simplistic, but it just meant so much to me. I was facing a very difficult communication with someone, and I had forgotten that life is joy. I can't tell you how much I appreciated that.

How to do the God-of-the-Heart reading

For the reading, you and your friend should sit across from each other at a comfortable distance. Decide who will be read first. The recipient will simply ground, own the room, and go into a receptive mode.

If you are the reader, ground, own the room, and be in the center of your head. With your eyes closed, look back behind the body of the person you are reading, and see, feel, or hear their God of the Heart. Say hello to your partner's God of the Heart. That energy will light you up and provide you with a great opportunity to clear your own pictures. Subsequently you begin by creating and destroying roses. The process, up to this point, should take only a minute or two. Then, in your mind say, "God of my partner's heart, what would you like my friend to know? What one thing would you like me to communicate to them on your behalf?" You may get your information fairly quickly, or you may have to be patient. Trust the first impression you get, then share what you perceive. If the God of the Heart says, "Everything is great!" simply communicate that. Should you get a picture of your friend and an older woman sitting stiffly across the table from each other, with your friend looking rather sad, you might ask your partner's God of the Heart, "What does this mean?" It might say, "Well, she has done some good forgiveness work with her mother, and now it's time to do some more."

Exploring barriers often uncovers very useful information

You may sometimes run into a psychic block that keeps you from seeing, feeling, or hearing anything. It's a good idea to assume that the block itself is a source of valuable information. Blow pictures and ask yourself whose resistance you are encountering, yours or your friend's. If it doesn't seem to be your block, you might say to your friend, "I'm not getting a great answer on this, maybe it's my resistance, maybe it's yours. Here's what I see." Then describe the block, what it looks like, feels like, sounds like. You can share your interpretation of the block or ask for your friend's thoughts. Exploring barriers often uncovers very useful information. Remember, if you find challenging aspects in your practice of any of these exercises, it is better to be resourceful than to have all kinds of resources.

Exercise 17: God-of-the-Heart reading

1. Resting your awareness in the center of your head, breathing gently and deeply, ground and own the room.
2. Say hello to your friend's God of the Heart.
3. Create and destroy roses.
4. Ask the God of the Heart for a message for your friend.
5. Thank your friend's God of the Heart.

6. Share what you perceived in that communication.
7. Continue to create and destroy roses.
8. Check that you are still grounded and owning the room.
9. Stand up, stretch, and reverse polarities.

The God-of-the-Heart conversation

The next exercise, the God-of-the-Heart conversation, is the most powerful means we know of to clear issues between you and another person. Within your God of the Heart, you can open up to your emotions and be more neutral toward them. From the God of the Heart and its resulting openness, you can communicate directly and deeply with another person's God of the Heart. Time and again, this exercise has proven itself.

Advanced Student: My father was terminally ill, and this past Christmas was the last time the whole family would be together. My family situation is always volatile. One of my sisters is an alcoholic, and my other sisters are very angry with her and blame her for everything, including my father's illness. So, about two weeks before I went home, I started doing God-of-the-Heart work with each one of my family members. With each God-of-the-Heart conversation, I could sense a very nice shift in the family dynamics. Anyway, it was wonderful. I am so grateful that my father's last Christmas with us was happy and peaceful.

The God-of-the-Heart conversation is much like an absentee reading, a reading performed at a distance with someone with whom you'd like to resolve an issue. To help you stay neutral and open to your growth, sit in your God of the Heart while having a conversation with the other person's God of the Heart. Ground and own the room, and connect to your God of the Heart. Imagine yourself becoming an amalgam with your God of the Heart, not dissolving into it, but being embraced by it. In that embrace, you'll find yourself more neutral, more loving, more filled with a sense of humor. The embrace doesn't have to be dramatic. It can be very subtle.

John: When getting into the God of the Heart, I just imagine myself lying back on big, white pillows full of wonderful God-of-the-Heart energy.

Even at the God-of-the-Heart level there isn't always agreement. Your partner's God of the Heart may say, "You're a darn so and so." From your God of the Heart, you can blow some pictures and say, "Okay, I'm listening." Then listen. After you've listened, communicate what you and your God of the Heart have to add. During your conversation, make it a point to remember your amusement and blow your own "issue" pictures.

John: Once something very amusing happened. I was using this technique with someone with whom I was having a lot of problems. I'd been doing it for about two weeks when, one morning, as I woke up, I heard her God of the Heart saying to me, "You know, you could do some changing, too." I had focused on "helping" her to change. I had been so locked in my own point of view that it hadn't occurred to me that I also might need to grow in the relationship.

In your conversation you must also be willing to listen and change. You will find that, from the God-of-the-Heart level, you are not perfect but that you are more capable. Change often takes time.

You can use this technique to finish what is unfinished

It can be very moving to use this technique with the deceased. People enjoy using this technique to say hello or to say their "good-byes"—to finish what was unfinished. The deceased often communicate in return, too. A student using this technique with her father was delighted to find that he was off on a new adventure. She said, "Hi Dad," and her father's God of the Heart replied, "I don't want to be Dad anymore." Then he turned into a young boy and related to her from that identity. Her father was in a period of time when he was exploring and learning about inner levels, and about the fuller and more complex nature of identity there.

You may explore the potential of this exercise to simply say hello to someone, or to assist in the evolution of challenging relationships. As you address your difficult relationships, remember that, often (maybe even usually), the most powerful healing technique you can use to heal people close to you is to figure out what they reflect in you, then heal that issue in yourself.

Exercise 18: *God-of-the-Heart conversation* **(absentee reading)**

1. Resting your awareness in the center of your head, ground and own the room, and breathe gently and deeply into your belly.
2. Go into your God of the Heart.
3. Say hello to someone's God of the Heart.
4. Create and destroy roses, remembering to clear the front and back.
5. Communicate your hello's, questions, or concerns.
6. Let the person's God of the Heart communicate back.
7. Continue to create and destroy roses.
8. Thank the God of the Heart.
9. Check that you are still grounded and owning the room.
10. Stand up, stretch, and reverse polarities.

Suggestions for Further Explorations

1. Become comfortable communicating with your God of the Heart. To deepen the naturalness and confidence of your relationship, practice communicating with your God of the Heart at least once a day for a week or two.

2. Explore and expand the God-of-the-Heart reading
   further with your friends. For example, ask to see
   past lives you've shared. You can create and destroy
   roses for any pictures that light up.
3. Choose a person with whom you would like to resolve an issue. Have a God-of-the-Heart conversation. Explore both points of view, and ask yourself
   how the issue is mirrored in you. Set a comfortable
   pace for yourself, with short sessions over a period of
   several days.

Chapter Five

Clairvoyance: A View from the Heart

Opening up to your clairvoyance can bring a powerful new intimacy, effectiveness, compassion, and playfulness to all that you do. For many of us, our natural intuitive and perceptive abilities, so intrinsically a part of who we are, have been misunderstood, closed down, and, in some unfortunate cases, declared perverse. In some ways, denying this aspect of ourselves is denying ourselves at the very heart of who we are. It could be said that, in opening our clairvoyance, we open a view from the heart, a view of our profound interconnectedness with each other and All That Is. We invite you to open up to and embrace your natural gifts, and to welcome back into your being a significant aspect of yourself.

While the whole body and aura are ultimately involved in the development of your clairvoyance, two areas stand out: the heart and the head. By concentrating on one or the other, you can probably succeed in developing your clairvoyance. But an easy, accurate clairvoyance requires both. Different people, however, may find one or the other an easier place to start.

The Heart's Clairvoyance

We have a few techniques to suggest for developing the heart's clairvoyance. More important than technique, however, is attitude. People who are genuinely nonjudgmental seem to have an easier time achieving clairvoyance. Being nonjudgmental is many people's goal but what does it mean? We find ourselves becoming judgmental when we think we understand another person's emotions or reasoning, or feel that we know what their emotions or reasoning should be. In fact, we have a saying: "A judgment is understanding another person from our own system." In other words, seeing someone through our own pictures.

Being nonjudgmental requires knowing our own feelings and opinions, and acting on them, while suspending the tendency to assume we know another's heart. Thus we can be responsible for our emotions and opinions and act on them, *and* honor the unknowable uniqueness of the other person. The exercises on neutrality (see chapter six, page 97) will aid you in releasing judgment and opening your heart.

For the following three heart-chakra meditations, you'll use a technique called "meditation by proxy." You can clear, heal, or observe anything by proxy. Here, you'll create a rose to be a "stand-in" for the energies of your heart, sixth, and crown chakras. Then you'll blow pictures, vacuum energy, and remove cords from the rose itself. You don't have to find the cords in your aura, because you can simply remove the cords from the rose. After you've cleared the rose, you can transform it in any way you like, until it has a more pleasing look, feel, or sound (or all three).

The heart chakra's clairvoyance

In this exercise, you will use a proxy rose to help you open up and clear the energy of your heart chakra's clairvoyance.

Exercise 19: *Clearing the heart chakra's clairvoyance*

1. Resting your awareness in the center of your head, breathe gently and deeply into your belly as you ground and own the room.
2. Create a rose in front of you and allow your heart chakra's clairvoyance to fill it.
3. Create and destroy roses for the pictures that light up related to your heart chakra's clairvoyance.

4. Remove cords from the rose itself.
5. Vacuum out any energy in your heart's clairvoyance that isn't yours.
6. Conclude by filling your rose with a nicer, lovelier, more comfortable color, sound, or feeling.
7. When you are pleased with how the energy looks, feels, or sounds, explode the rose and bring its energy back into your crown chakra and allow the energy to flow down your back and into your heart.
8. Run some energy.
9. Check to see that you are still grounded and owning the room.
10. When ready, stand up, stretch, and reverse polarities.

Harmonizing your heart and crown chakras

A very important aspect of clairvoyance is the harmony between the heart and the crown chakras. To "harmonize" your heart and crown chakras, create a rose for each chakra, clear their energy, then make any changes you feel might increase their harmony.[1]

Exercise 20: *Harmonizing the heart and crown chakras*

1. Resting your awareness in the center of your head, breathe gently and deeply into your belly as you ground and own the room.
2. Create a rose and let your heart chakra's energy fill it.
3. Create and destroy roses for any pictures the rose lights up. Remove cords from your heart-chakra rose, vacuum out any energy that isn't yours, and move the rose one foot to your left.

---

[1] This exercise was inspired by the meditation on the twin hearts. Choa Kok Sui, *Pranic Healing* (York Beach, Maine: Samuel Weiser, 1990), pp. 235–244.

4. Create another rose and let your crown-chakra energy fill it.
5. Create and destroy roses for any pictures the rose lights up. Remove cords from your crown-chakra rose, vacuum out any energy that isn't yours, and move the rose one foot to your right.
6. Observe the roses side by side for a moment, then make any changes you'd like in order to increase their harmony with one another.
7. When you are pleased with their energy, explode the heart chakra rose and bring its energy back through your crown, down your back, and into your heart chakra.
8. Explode the crown-chakra rose and bring its energy back into your crown.
9. Run some energy.
10. Check to see that you are still grounded and owning the room.
11. When ready, stand up, stretch, and reverse polarities.

Harmonizing your heart and sixth chakras

The connection between the heart chakra and the sixth chakra will be very important to your clairvoyance. The culture has set up a dichotomy between the heart and the head, but for your clairvoyance you'll want a nice balance of the two energies.

To harmonize the heart and sixth chakra you can create a rose for each, then imagine a line connecting and harmonizing them. If they are out of phase with each other you probably won't even be able to connect them. When a line can rest comfortably between them, and they look, feel or sound in harmony, then you'll do well. Let the heart energy go into the heart, and the sixth-chakra energy go back into the sixth. Then let the energy of the line remain flexible and come into the body as well. It's the energy of the connection that is important, not the line itself. The energy between them lets you coordinate the head's and the heart's clairvoyance.

Exercise 21: *Harmonizing the heart and sixth chakras*

1. Resting your awareness in the center of your head, breathe gently and deeply into your belly as you ground and own the room.
2. Create a rose and let your heart chakra's energy fill it. Create and destroy roses.
3. Remove cords from your rose, vacuum out any energy that isn't yours, and move the rose one foot to your left.
4. Create another rose and let your sixth-chakra energy fill it. Create and destroy roses.
5. Remove cords from your sixth-chakra rose, vacuum out any energy that isn't yours, and move the rose one foot to your right.
6. Observe the roses side by side. Then let a line connect them comfortably.
7. Allow them to look, feel, or sound in harmony.
8. When you are pleased with their harmony explode the roses and bring the heart energy through your crown chakra, down your back, and into your heart chakra.
9. Bring your sixth-chakra energy directly through your crown and into your sixth chakra.
10. Let the energy of the connection rest flexibly between the chakras.
11. Explode your picture blowing roses and recycle the energy.
12. Run some energy.
13. Check to see that you are still grounded and owning the room.
14. When ready, stand up, stretch, and reverse polarities.

The Head: The Pineal Gland, Rational Mind, and the Pituitary Gland

Three major functions instrumental in the development of your clairvoyance are the etheric processes associated with your pineal gland, your rational mind, and your pituitary gland. You'll use the physical locations as a reference point,

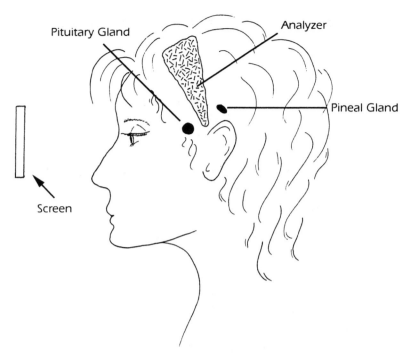

Figure 5. Pituitary gland, pineal gland, and analyzer.

but your focus will be the spiritual energy related to each organ, rather than the organ itself (see figure 5).

The pineal gland: the center of your head

Getting in touch with the distinctive energies of the pineal gland, rational mind, and pituitary gland will help you find the powerful calm place we call the center of the head, which is the seat of your personal soul. From the center of your head emanates a distinct, calm, "knowing" energy that is nestled in and around your pineal gland. The pineal gland is located roughly between, and a little above, the ears. Clairvoyantly, the pineal gland's energy is seen as an angled oval.

The center of the head has such a lovely, neutral energy that we encourage you to focus your awareness in the center of your head most of the time, especially during psychic work.

Your clairvoyance is significantly enhanced when you rest your awareness in the center of your head and "look" out through your third eye, the pituitary complex.

The rational mind: the analyzer

If you move your attention a little forward from the pineal gland, you enter a wedge of spiritual energy constituting the rational mind called the "analyzer," roughly 4 inches wide and 2½ inches tall, located at the top of the skull and tapering down to a wedge at about mid-temple, at the level of the bridge of the nose.

It is important, in developing your clairvoyance, to be able to recognize the analyzer's energy, because placing your awareness in the analyzer can actually block your clairvoyance. Moreover, it's important to blow pictures when in the analyzer, because failing to do so can cause people headaches. Since the analyzer, the frequent haunt of the intellectual, can often be identified by its "serious" or intense energy, it can be very helpful to explore these locations while in a relaxed, open, and playful mood. Your analyzer is vital and has very complex psychic functions. Trying to explain them would take us away from this book's purposes. Suffice it to say that, clairvoyance requires a flexible, easygoing, and expansive energy. Those who spend a lot of time in their analyzers can have a more difficult time opening to their clairvoyance.

The pituitary gland: your third eye

The famous third eye is a complex of energy surrounding the pituitary gland. The psychic influence of the pituitary flows forward to the forehead chakra between the eyebrows. People often describe the pituitary as having a subtle energy, peaceful and feminine. You'll be more clairvoyant when the forehead chakra is open and the pituitary gland is energized. The pituitary gland is just a little in front of and a little below the bottom of the analyzer. Another way to find the pituitary's energy is to close your eyes and "rest" your gaze at the bridge of your nose (where the frame of eyeglasses rests). Seen clairvoyantly, the pituitary is much like a green pea located an inch or two behind the center of the eyebrows.

Exploring the pineal gland, the pituitary gland, and the analyzer

In the first exercise for opening your clairvoyance, you will explore the differences between these three psychic energies. You can use the physical locations of the pineal gland, the analyzer, and the pituitary gland as reference points for their spiritual energy. Each location will have its own unique feel to it.

Begin the exercise by closing your eyes and resting your awareness in the center of your head. Feel the distinct calm.[2] While breathing gently, ground and own the room, then continue to breathe deeply. Relax for about 30 seconds.

One of the most useful skills you can bring to your clairvoyance is an ability to relax and let your eyes become still. After you've reached a relaxed state, you can begin to blow pictures and move forward from the pineal into the denser energy of your analyzer. Observe how different from the pineal energy it feels. Though most people experience the analyzer as an intense, concentrated energy, by continuing to blow pictures, you will eventually clear it sufficiently for it to become more comfortable and less dense, even though it retains its essential linear rationality.

Next, move slightly forward and down from your analyzer into the energy of the pituitary gland. First hone in on the pituitary gland itself, then move your attention to the forehead, at the brow chakra, and explore the energy there. (The two similar energies of the pituitary gland and the forehead chakra constitute the pituitary complex.) Alternate back and forth between the two locations (the pituitary itself and the brow) and continue blowing pictures.

---

[2]It is possible to have so much energy from other people in the center of your head that the calmness is hard to find. As you continue clearing your aura, sooner or later you will find the calmness.

Now move back and forth between all three locations, the pineal, the analyzer, and the pituitary (which includes the forehead chakra and the pituitary gland itself), until you can distinguish—by seeing, feeling, hearing, or imagining—the three distinct energies. Conclude the exercise by returning to the center of your head.

Exercise 22: *Exploring the pineal area, the pituitary area, and the analyzer*

1. Close your eyes, rest your awareness in the center of your head, breathe gently and deeply into your belly, as you ground and own the room.
2. Relax for about 30 seconds in the quiet and calm energy of the center of your head.
3. Create roses and begin to blow the pictures lighting up in your head, front and back.
4. Move your attention forward toward the temple into your analyzer and explore the energy of the analyzer for about 20 seconds.
5. Continue to create and destroy roses.
6. Allow your attention to move forward and a little down from your analyzer, into your pituitary gland, and explore the energy of the pituitary for about 30 seconds.
7. Move back and forth between the pituitary and the forehead chakras for about 30 seconds.
8. Move all the way back into the center of your head.
9. Remembering your amusement, repeat the sequence until you can distinguish the three energies.
10. When finished rest in and "own" the calm center of your head.
11. Create and destroy some more roses, recycling your energy.
12. Run some refreshing Earth and cosmic energy.
13. When ready, stand up, stretch, and reverse polarities.

Increasing clairvoyance: clearing and running energy

This exercise will help you open your clairvoyance by clearing and energizing your pineal, analyzer, and pituitary complex. We'll go through the steps, then you can use the outline to go through the exercise at your leisure.

First, ground and own the room and, at each of the three locations, blow pictures, vacuum energy, remove cords, and give each organ a small grounding cord. The grounding cord can be like a laser beam, half the diameter of a drinking straw, or smaller.

Next, clear and invigorate the pineal and pituitary with blue and gold cosmic energies. From above your crown, allow golden cosmic energy to shine into your pineal gland. Let it "charge" for about 30 seconds, then allow that golden cosmic energy to turn and flow forward through the pituitary and out through the brow chakra to the horizon. Let it continue to flow as you move on to the next step.

To invigorate your pituitary, imagine a cosmic sapphire-blue energy streaming from the horizon, flowing into your brow chakra and into your pituitary. Let it "charge" the pituitary for about 30 seconds. Then let the blue cosmic energy turn and flow up into the pineal, and continue out through the crown chakra to the cosmos. Let these two streams continue to flow, mixing and playing, for about one minute.

Exercise 23: *Clearing and running energy*

1. Breathing gently and deeply into your belly, ground and own the room, and let yourself become still for about 30 seconds.
2. Find the energy of your pineal gland and create and destroy roses.
3. Remove cords from it, create a vacuum-cleaner rose and remove other people's energy, give your pineal gland its own grounding cord, and fill it with the energy of a golden sun.
4. Find the energy of your analyzer, and create and destroy roses.

5. Remove cords from it, create a vacuum-cleaner rose and remove energy, give your analyzer its own grounding cord, and fill it with the energy of a golden sun.
6. Find the energy of your pituitary gland and create and destroy roses.
7. Remove cords from it, create a vacuum-cleaner rose and remove other people's energy, give your pituitary gland its own grounding cord, and fill it with a beautiful ball of sapphire-blue cosmic energy.
8. From a foot above your head, let a golden light shine down into the pineal for a moment, then let that golden light turn and flow though the pituitary and out to the horizon. Let it continue to flow.
9. From out on the horizon, let a beam of sapphire-blue cosmic light shine through your brow chakra and into your pituitary for a moment, then allow that blue light to flow into your pineal, turn, and flow out through the top of your head.
10. Let those two streams mix and play for about 30 seconds.
11. Create and destroy roses and recycle your energy.
12. Check that you are still grounded and owning the room.
13. When ready, stand up, stretch, and reverse polarities.

Overlapping the fields of the pituitary and the pineal

Allowing the fields of your pineal and pituitary glands to "charge-up" and overlap will stimulate your clairvoyance considerably. This process builds on the previous exercise, differing only in that you will expand the cosmic gold and blue energies of the pineal and pituitary glands to a sphere 2 to 3½ inches in diameter before releasing them.

Exercise 24: *Overlapping the fields of the pineal and pituitary*

1. Breathe gently and deeply into your belly, ground and own the room, and allow yourself to relax.

2. Create and destroy roses throughout the exercise.
3. Find the energy of your pineal gland. Then allow golden cosmic energy to flow from above your head into the pineal gland, and energize it.
4. Let the energy increase in intensity for about 30 seconds, allowing the intensified energy to form a sphere around the pineal 2 to 3½ inches in diameter.
5. Allow the sphere to remain in place and move your attention to your pituitary gland.
6. Find the energy of your pituitary gland. Then let a beam of sapphire-blue light from out on the horizon shine through your brow chakra and into your pituitary, energizing it.
7. Let the energy increase in intensity for about 30 seconds. Then allow the intensified energy to create a sphere around the pituitary 2 to 3½ inches in diameter.
8. Allow the two spheres of cosmic gold and cosmic blue to overlap each other for about 1 minute, or for as long as is comfortable.
9. Release each stream to mix and join with the other, allowing the cosmic gold to continue out to the horizon and the cosmic blue to flow out of the crown to the cosmos for about 60 seconds.
10. Allow your awareness to remain in the center of your head.
11. Check that you are still grounded and owning the room.
12. When ready, stand up, stretch, and reverse polarities.

Stimulating the pineal gland

It is said that the pineal gland begins to calcify and become rigid in most of us by about the age of six. Your clairvoyance will be enhanced by the psychic stimulation of your pineal gland. You can playfully imagine a miniature of yourself sitting behind your pineal gland, gently massaging the gland for about 10 seconds. Remember, you are healing the physical pineal gland and also charging up the higher, nonphysical frequencies of the gland. Allow the energy to flow softly out into your head, then into your entire body and aura.

Note: Do this exercise only in moderation. If overdone, one could get a headache.

Exercise 25: *Stimulating the pineal gland*

1. Resting your awareness in the center of your head, breathe gently into your belly, ground, and own the room.
2. Begin to create and destroy roses.
3. Imagine a miniature of yourself sitting behind your pineal gland, gently massaging it for about 10 seconds, and allow a glow to fill the pineal gland and the ball of fluid that surrounds it.
4. Allow the energy generated by this activity to flow gently into your head and throughout your body.
5. Breathe slowly and gently into your belly for about one minute.
6. Leisurely repeat this complete cycle twice, remembering to breathe gently for one minute between cycles.
7. When finished, remain in the center of your head, and ground and own the room.
8. Then stand up, stretch, and reverse polarities.

Clairvoyant Screens

As you know, the light you see with your eyes proceeds from the object you are observing through the lens of your eye, and onto your retina. The brain then interprets what appears on the screen of the retina. Components of your spiritual anatomy, called "screens" are similar to the retina. Using your screens, you can effectively "see" and read psychic information. To most people, these screens appear as rectangular and very similar to a movie screen.

Though you have many screens, we will work with one in particular that is utilized for clairvoyance. It is located four to twelve inches in front of your forehead. You can access it with your eyes either open or closed, though it may be easier to "see" by closing your eyes. As you become more adept, you can practice using your screen with your eyes both open and closed. The sizes of these screens vary quite a bit, so you may find your screen is 4 by 6 inches, 8 by 10 inches, or possibly larger.

You'll get greater psychic detail by using your screen, and it is an unintrusive way to read energy when working with others. If you neglect to use a screen while reading others, you may pull their energy into your second chakra, which, as you may recall, this system discourages.

Using a screen is easy. For example, if you want to look at the energy of one of your chakras, simply ask the energy of that chakra to appear on your screen and allow the detail to fill in. Or you can ask your whole aura to appear on your screen and ask to see any stuck energy, or cords, or whatever information you'd like to access.

Locating your psychic screen

The following exercise will help you locate your psychic screen. First clear and energize your hand chakras, then use your hands to find your screen, which is probably 4 to 12 inches out in front of your forehead. The distance varies. With your eyes closed, extend your hand far out in front of your forehead, then slowly bring it toward you, until you sense it "bumping" into the very subtle energy of your screen (see figure 5, page 80).

Exercise 26: *Locating your psychic screen*

1. Resting your awareness in the center of your head, relax, breathe gently and deeply into your belly, as you ground and own the room.
2. Create and destroy roses.

3. Begin with your hand far out in front of you and slowly bring it toward you, until you "feel" or sense your screen.
4. Move your hand back and forth, noticing the energy of your screen.
5. Run some energy, and check your grounding when finished.

Create a screen if you can't locate one

After some exploration, if you feel you can't find a screen, create one for yourself. Eventually, you'll probably find more screens, or create screens wherever you want. In fact, some systems advocate creating and destroying screens after each reading. The very act of creating a screen can actually help to increase your clairvoyance.

Cleaning and repairing your psychic screen

Often, your screen will need to be repaired and cleaned. It may be pushed out of place or broken, and it will most likely be dirty. Energy, cords, and pictures may accumulate on, around and behind your screen from this and many lifetimes, so clean all the nooks and crannies too. Energize your screen with a golden sun, then let it settle into its own color. And finally, it is helpful to ground your screen. When finished cleaning and grounding, "own" your unique vision by affirming silently to yourself, "My screen." It is often very interesting to see what lights up when you start clearing your clairvoyance.

Advanced student: When I first began to clear my psychic screens I was very surprised to find my grandfather's pictures there—everything "seen" was in reference to his success.

Another student: It was hard for me to see anything at first. When I started clearing my psychic screen, "rules" lit up about not being allowed to use my clairvoyance. I blew roses, and removed cords and energy every day for a week, then my clairvoyance began to open up quite a bit.

Exercise 27: *Cleaning and repairing your screen*

1. Resting your awareness in the center of the head, breathe gently and deeply into your belly, and ground and own the room.
2. Relax and allow your eyes to become still.
3. Create and destroy roses.
4. Imagine you can see your screen, adjust and straighten it, and using a soft cloth, clean both sides.
5. Vacuum out any energy that is not yours and blow any pictures that are on it.
6. Remove cords from your screen, front and back, and use your imagination to repair any damage you find.
7. Charge your screen with a golden sun, and allow it then to settle into its own color.
8. Give it its own grounding cord.
9. Affirm silently to yourself, "My screen."
10. Continue to create and destroy roses.
11. Run some energy.
12. When through, stand up, stretch, and reverse polarities.

Reading from your screen

After repairing and cleaning your screen, practice giving yourself a reading. Explore the possibilities of seeing with your eyes both open and closed. It is often easier to see more with your eyes closed than open. Most people prefer one style or the other, though you may find you'll use a combination of both.

To practice using your screen, close your eyes, locate your screen, then ask for one particular chakra to light up on it. Breathe gently, blow pictures, and allow your eyes to become very still and relaxed as the detail fills in. Explore and play with the image. Practice turning the image to see it from several different angles, or even use your imagination to heal it. Have fun.

Exercise 28: *Reading from your screen*

1. Close your eyes, rest your awareness in the center of your head, breathe gently and deeply into your belly, and ground and own the room.
2. Relax and allow your eyes to become very still.
3. Create and destroy roses.
4. Find your screen and ask a chakra to appear on it.
5. Relax and allow the details to fill in; explore the image; heal it with your imagination.
6. Repeat this sequence with another chakra if you like.
7. Continue to create and destroy roses.
8. When finished, explode all the remaining pictures on your screen
9. Run some energy.
10. When through, stand up, stretch and reverse polarities.

Measuring the distance between the sixth-chakra energies

Many of the earlier exercises for developing clairvoyance (the psychic sense of seeing) can be done by using your clairsentience (the psychic sense of feeling). By doing those exercises, you will activate the psychic energies of clairvoyance, even if you are using clairsentience to do the activation. At some point in the development process, everyone learns to use psychic energies in a visual way. The following exercise helps enormously in developing the skill to use the sixth-chakra energies in a visual style. In earlier exercises, you took your attention to those other parts. The key here is to keep your attention in the center of your head and look out from there to see your analyzer, your pituitary, and your psychic screen.

First work with your analyzer, then with your pituitary, then with your psychic screen. Ground, own the room, and bring your awareness into the center of your head. From the center of your head, measure the distance to your analyzer. After you've measured the distance, look, from where you are in the center of your head, through that distance to your analyzer. Repeat these steps for the pituitary and the psychic screen. You may or may not see much. The important thing is to imagine a sense of distance.

Exercise 29: *Measuring the distance between the sixth-chakra energies*

1. Bring your awareness to the center of your head, breathe gently and deeply into your belly as you ground and own the room.
2. Create and destroy roses.
3. Keeping your awareness focused in the center of your head, measure—see, feel, or hear—the distance between the center of your head and your analyzer. (Give the distance a number to make it seem more real to you.)
4. When you've noted the distance, remain in the center of your head and look through that distance to the analyzer for 10 to 30 seconds.
5. When you've completed the exercise with the analyzer, continue to create and destroy roses and check your grounding.
6. "Measure" the distance between the center of your head and your pituitary gland, and look through that distance to the pituitary gland. Then repeat the process for the screen out in front of your forehead.
7. Run some Earth and cosmic energy.
8. Check to see that you are still grounded and owning the room.
9. When finished, stand up, stretch, and reverse polarities.

Breathing into the pituitary and the pineal

A very simple and effective way to clear and increase your clairvoyance is to gently and slowly "breathe" into your pineal and pituitary glands and observe your breath, breathing your energy in and releasing energies that are not yours with each exhalation. For many people, intoning "Om" increases this exercise's effectiveness and power.[3]

Focusing on the tip of your nose

Another great exercise we suggest you explore is to gently focus on the tip of your nose with your eyes opened. This will help you release tension and allow the eye muscles to relax. The key is to learn to focus gently on the tip of the nose. You must be careful to do this exercise in moderation to avoid a headache or strained eye muscles. Allow the amount of time you hold the focus on your nose to gradually build over a period of weeks.

Allowing your eyes to become still increases depth

Allowing your eyes to become very still increases the vibrancy of colors, the detail of your images, the depth of your information, and your receptiveness. When you want this depth, you can close your eyes, breathe deeply and smoothly, and take the time needed to let your eyes become very still. Let your physical eyes relax so that your mind's eye can see.

Gloria: I've had to learn how to become very still while giving a reading. When I become intent about "getting" information, my whole body tenses up, and I lose everything. It's as if I hit the delete button on my computer by accident—my screen literally goes blank. I have to allow myself to stop, let go of the moment's seriousness, breathe, and relax back into the information.

As much fun as it is to be able to access psychic information, it seems fun and important to explore the state of being still—not seeking information, but stillness itself.

---

[3] Breathing through your chakras is also a great way to clean them, breathing your energy into the chakras, and exhaling any energy that is not yours.

Using a gauge

Many psychics, both beginners and experienced readers, find that validating or clarifying their psychic information can be made easier by using a versatile tool called a "psychic gauge" (see figure 6, below). There are numerous ways in which you can work with a gauge. A very simple and effective approach is to create one to help you clarify a yes or no answer. Another very useful approach is to ask a gauge to help you approximate percentages. For example, when you find a belief

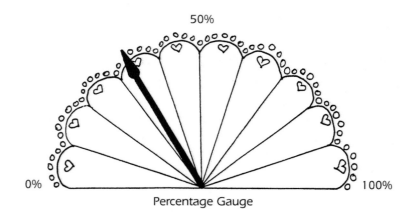

Percentage Gauge

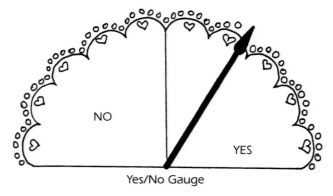

Yes/No Gauge

Figure 6. Gauges.

in your aura, you can create a gauge to show you what percentage of that belief is your personal energy and what percentage is someone else's energy. Remove the energy which isn't yours from the belief and you'll find the belief much easier to change and improve.

Suggestions for Further Explorations

1. To practice opening your heart's clairvoyance, choose someone with whom you disagree and, while practicing nonjudgment and releasing any need to change them, simply "see" their point of view with your clairvoyance.
2. Imagine an image appearing on your psychic screen and let the detail fill in. Practice zooming in for a close-up of your face, your eyes, your hands, or your chakras, then zoom out. Have your image turn around and repeat the exercise with your back.
3. Locate and clean some of your other psychic screens. To find your screens you might find it helpful to close your eyes and notice where you "look" for information in your mind and aura. Many people find a screen on the brow, and another just in front of the pituitary gland.

Chapter Six

The Compassionate State: Neutrality

The gentle state of neutrality, one of the most power-ful and effective tools for dealing with difficult situations, is at the core of our practice. Neutrality is creating an emotional openness that allows you to release your resistance to your experiences. You simply observe and allow experience to be just what it is, without judging it, without having to change it. Neutrality, in very subtle ways, creates a framework of compassion for yourself and others.

Neutrality and Growth

It is said that 95 percent of our growth can occur without using any technique other than neutrality.[1] Far from being the absence of emotion, neutrality is an opening up to the complexity, subtlety, and multidimensionality of emotions and experience. When you gain a neutral perspective, you become more "present" and effective, your understanding deepens, and many of your issues resolve. The profound, though subtle, significance and complexities of relationships make much more sense. Increased compassion for yourself and others becomes possible.

---

[1]John first heard this percentage in a lecture by John Fulton, long a respected teacher at BPI (the psychic training institute founded by Lewis Bostwick), and now director of Aesclepion Institute. Much of the information underlying this book comes from tapes produced by BPI or Aesclepion Institute.

Before practicing neutrality, let's take a few minutes to observe what it feels like not to be in neutrality.

Intentionally lighting yourself up

The technique you'll use to achieve a non-neutral state is called "lighting yourself up." All you need to do is think of something that has an emotional "charge" for you, then allow all the pictures associated with that issue to intensify and "light up" in your aura for a moment. This intensification should enable you to become much more aware of the pictures in your space as they begin to energize. Knowing how to light yourself up, and recognizing when you are *naturally* "lit up," is a powerful mechanism for acknowledging and releasing psychic/emotional blocks from your aura. Please take one or two minutes now to experience what being "lit up" feels like before you begin the neutrality exercises.

Exercise 30: *Lighting yourself up*

1. Resting your awareness in the center of your head, breathe gently and deeply into your belly.
2. Close your eyes and create a rose in front of you.
3. Imagine a picture of something that annoys you and place the annoying picture on your rose.
4. Without changing or fixing it, allow your aura to fill with the varied emotions and pictures that "light up" in your space related to your annoying picture.
5. Allow those intensifying pictures and emotions to build for one or two minutes, simply noticing your body, your breathing, your emotions, just "allowing" them.
6. When you feel "lit up," ground, own the room, and explode all those pictures.
7. Thank your body for being so willing to change, and run some Earth and cosmic energy.
8. When you're ready, stand up, stretch, and reverse polarities.

Cultivating neutrality:
compassion for yourself and others

Three significant yet basic practices will help you cultivate neutrality. The first, which you touched on in the previous exercise, is to simply "allow" life, to openly observe and accept life without judgment—discernment, but not judgment. We call this "spacious observation" because of the "space" it gives the event or issue. The second practice cultivates and honors the recognition that *all* experience is sacred, and that *all* experience fosters growth. We call this "recognizing all experience as sacred." The third practice, "setting your crown to gold," is allowing your crown chakra to vibrate at the compassionate and "open" frequency of gold, the most nonjudgmental frequency that you can run in your crown as a human. When you set your crown to gold, you create a more resourceful, receptive, and compassionate state in yourself.

The subtle understanding and effective state of neutrality grows with practice. Never static and ever-evolving, neutrality does not require completion or perfection, just openness.

Spacious observation: acceptance

For the first exercise in neutrality, spacious observation, think of an event or issue that annoys you and lights you up. When something annoys you, it tends to "get in your face." When you look at it with your mind's eye, it tends to insinuate itself into your face or aura and not move easily. Without judging or changing it, allow yourself to observe it just where and as it is. Say hello to any judgment of it or need to "fix" it. Be sure to first acknowledge any feelings, then allow them also to light up pictures which you explode as they arise. Delay exploding your picture of the event or issue itself, just continue observing it, keeping your space clear by exploding any pictures that light up. Space will develop spontaneously between you and your picture of the event or issue.

When it does your breath will relax. Continue to breathe gently and deeply as you create and destroy roses for the pictures, which light up. When you can look at the picture and breathe comfortably and deeply without forcing yourself, you will be in a good state of neutrality.

For this exploration, continue working with the annoying picture from the previous exercise if it still holds a charge, or choose another annoying issue or event. Let your picture light up. Then openly observe it for 5 to 10 minutes (or for as long as seems appropriate), until you feel more "space" between you and your issue, and your breath relaxes.

Exercise 31: *Spacious observation: acceptance*

1. Resting your awareness in the center of your head, breathe gently and deeply into your belly, as you ground and own the room.
2. Close your eyes and create a rose in front of you.
3. Imagine a picture of something that annoys you and place that annoying picture on your rose.
4. Delay exploding that picture. Instead allow that picture to light you up. Say hello to any judgment and keep your aura clear by exploding any pictures that light up those feelings in your aura.
5. Continue just looking at the annoying picture until you see or feel space develop between you and the picture.
6. Notice your breath relax and deepen into your belly.
7. Just "allow" your emotions.
8. When you feel more relaxed and at ease with the annoying picture, run some Earth and cosmic energy.
9. Thank your body for being so willing and adventurous.
10. When you're ready, stand up, stretch, and reverse polarities.

Recognizing all experience as sacred: perspective and growth

The second practice in neutrality cultivates two powerful yet simple intents—recognizing all experience as sacred, and appreciating all experience as an opportunity for growth.

Exploration of these deceptively simple concepts can be deeply life-changing. When you cultivate the understanding that all experience is sacred and that all experience is an opportunity for growth, every experience—good, bad, or indifferent—can unveil its gracefulness and meaning. This allows appreciation and compassion for yourself and others to deepen.

For this exercise, recall another annoying picture and let it light you up as before. Consider the possibility that, in some way, you helped create the event or issue for learning purposes. Understand, imagine, or pretend that, at an energy level, you collaborated in setting up the event or issue so that you might practice one of the assignments you gave yourself before birth. From that perspective, ask yourself a few pertinent questions, such as, "What do I want this event or issue to teach me about myself?" Or, "What does this event or issue teach me about my relationships?" Or possibly, "What does my Higher Self hope I will learn from this?" (This may light you up, so be sure to continue blowing pictures.)

Cultivating such a perspective will strengthen and nourish your neutrality and your appreciation of the sacredness and multiplicity of experience. Cultivating such a perspective will create more space for compassion toward yourself and others.

Exercise 32: *Recognizing all experience as sacred: growth*

1. Resting your awareness in the center of your head, breathe gently and deeply into your belly, as you ground and own the room.
2. Close your eyes and create a rose in front of you.
3. Imagine a picture of something that annoys or disturbs you, and place that picture on your rose.
4. Without changing or fixing it, observe your picture.
5. Create and destroy roses for any associated pictures that light up in your aura.
6. Continue to breathe gently and deeply into your belly.

7. Ask yourself, and/or your Higher Self, what wisdom your picture offers, what it teaches you about yourself? This will most likely light you up.
8. Continue to create and destroy roses, check your grounding, and own the room.
9. Notice your body, your breathing, your emotions, and just "allow" them.
10. When you feel as if you have insight, sit with it and breathe gently and deeply into your belly for a moment.
11. Thank your body and run some energy.
12. When you're ready, stand up, stretch, and reverse polarities.

Setting your crown to gold: neutrality

Gloria: One morning upon arriving "on time" for what I thought was a 9:30 AM meeting, I was met in the hall by a man who was very angry with me for missing the meeting. With an icy politeness, he informed me that they had their meeting two hours earlier without me. Then he went on sarcastically, "Do you think we should try to gather everyone from their busy schedules *now* for *your* convenience?"

As he loomed over me, waiting for my response, I took about five seconds to check my grounding, own the room, and set my crown color to gold. I calmly replied, "Of course not," and then apologized for my misunderstanding, and for having inconvenienced everyone. Clearly this man was justified in being upset with me. But I felt that his demeanor was way out of line. It had, after all, been an unfortunate but honest mistake.

But the moment was intriguing. It was the first time that I'd ever been able to psychically "see" an interaction, and I began to "see" how he expected me to respond. His expectations appeared as different colored energies in his aura—energies that seemed to imply that I should cringe and grovel. It was fascinating. But most rewarding was the fact that neutrality allowed me to stay grounded and not respond to his intimidation. Despite the awkwardness of the circumstance, I felt surprisingly clear and centered, and was pleased with my interactions with such an angry and powerful man.

The frequency of your crown chakra determines the tone and the resourcefulness with which you interact with the world. The third practice in cultivating neutrality is to consciously set your crown chakra to vibrate at the frequency of gold, the most effective color to run in your crown for increased neutrality. Setting your crown to gold will help you reach the receptive, resourceful, and nonjudgmental state of neutrality almost effortlessly. And it's easy. After you ground and own the room, allow your attention to focus on your crown, create a golden rose in front of your forehead, then allow your crown chakra to match that lovely golden color.

Exercise 33: *Setting your crown to gold: neutrality*

1. Resting your awareness in the center of your head, breathe gently and deeply into your belly as you ground and own the room.
2. Close your eyes and create a rose in front of you.
3. Imagine a picture of something that concerns or worries you and place it on your rose.
4. Without changing or fixing it, observe your picture for a moment, allowing it to light you up.
5. Continue to breathe gently and deeply into your belly, create a lovely golden rose on your screen, and allow your crown chakra to match that lovely golden color.
6. Notice your body, your breathing, your emotions, your resourcefulness, and your receptivity as your crown becomes more golden and neutral.
7. Begin to create and destroy roses.
8. Observe your picture until you feel more resourceful and open to the experience. Your crown may lose its golden color, so you may need to reset it to gold.

9. Destroy all of the pictures and recycle your energy.
10. Thank your body and run some energy.
11. When you're ready, stand up, stretch, and reverse polarities.

Increasing your ability to respond to experiences

As you practice neutrality, you increase your ability to respond to all kinds of emotions, experiences, and memories, and open to all joys and pain, releasing each emotion when it has been experienced and fulfilled. If you can remember what it feels like to be neutral about something, you can just repeat that feeling with new experiences. Neutrality does not mean not feeling, it means not judging that feeling. You can use all feelings to inform yourself and, from neutrality, you can gain more resourcefulness in how to react.

A *positive event seen in neutrality reveals more*

Have your ever had an experience that was so good that you almost hyperventilated? When you just sit in neutrality and begin to watch your responses to a positive event, you'll probably see a lot of other aspects of the event. Ordinarily, we use names and labels to distance ourselves unintentionally from our experiences. We relate to the label and not the experience. Clairvoyantly, this shows up as responding to pictures in your aura rather than the external events themselves. To explore the possibility of having missed the subtleties of an event by labeling it, recall a positive experience, set your crown to gold, and observe the experience for a while. Notice if there is more to the picture than meets the eye, or label.

Exercise 34: *A pleasant picture when seen in neutrality*

1. Resting your awareness in the center of your head, breathe gently and deeply into your belly as you ground and own the room.
2. Begin to create and destroy roses.

3. Create a rose in front of you and let a picture of a pleasant experience come onto it.
4. Set your crown to gold, and observe the pleasant experience from neutrality for a while.
5. Blow up your pleasant picture and rose.
6. Thank your body and replenish your aura.
7. When ready, stand up, stretch, and reverse polarities.

Neutrality is the position of greatest emotions

To summarize, you're not in neutrality if you're unable to feel, if you have moved beyond feelings, if you have transcended feeling. Neutrality is an opening up to the complexity, subtlety, and multidimensionality of emotion.

Neutrality is never substituted for any emotion. Neutrality allows you to put the emotion into the bigger picture, and to learn to cherish the richness of the whole emotional event. When you genuinely appreciate that complexity and that richness, you won't get stuck on any piece of the emotion or go into resistance to the emotion. Neutrality is, in fact, the position of greatest emotions. What we have, as a culture, often identified as intense emotion is actually the truncating of emotion, the artificial narrowing of emotion by ignoring its complexity. Often, what we imagine to be intensity is just the introduction of resistance into emotions. In fact, our definition of intense emotion usually requires that we be in resistance to it.

And, of course, you have to jump into the paradox that you can be in neutrality about your resistance to something. If a person is in denial about the resistance they feel to an experience, and they feel an enforced feeling of calm, then they're actually in resistance. But, if they're in neutrality around their resistance, if they allow and are open to their resistance, or even repulsion, then they're in a kind of neutrality.

Responsibility and Blame

Neutrality requires taking responsibility for your emotions. If you're blaming someone else without some humor or neutrality around the blaming process, then you're not in neutrality, you're in resistance. If you're blaming someone and you have some humor and neutrality around the process of blaming them, if you're simultaneously and complexly aware that you are responsible for your own experience, then you can be in a kind of neutrality. Your emotions will flow smoothly and you will be resourceful with them.

From neutrality, you can still experience pain and anger, but you can experience them as emotions that are moving through you. You can experience them in a way that validates your emotions, in a way that can be experienced and expressed in your body and your life, in a way that takes responsibility for creating your own reality, in a way that is more complex than the simple narrowing of the field of your experience into what's "wrong" with the other person.

Associating into a picture

When someone agonizes over an event and has a difficult time gaining neutrality around an issue, they are often "associated into" their picture and stuck in past experience. One can often gain relief and perspective by merely stepping out of the picture—by seeing, hearing, feeling, tasting, or smelling, from outside, rather than from inside the picture.

To make a problematic picture more manageable it is often enough to project the experience on a screen outside of your aura, observe yourself from "outside" of the scene (that is, so that you can see over the back of your own head), and then explode the picture. Particularly intense or traumatic experiences may require moving your screen fifty feet away or repeating the exercise over a period of time.

Exercise 35: *Observing yourself from outside of a picture*

1. Rest your awareness in the center of your head, breathe gently and deeply into your belly, and ground and own the room.
2. Destroy the pictures that light up.

3. Create a screen at a comfortable distance outside of your aura and invite an image to appear from which you'd like to disassociate.
4. Practice viewing it from outside the scene (from behind yourself, so that you can observe the scene from over the back of your own head).
5. Pace yourself. Blow pictures and allow your breathing to stabilize.
6. When the picture loses its charge, enjoy exploding it and bringing yourself into current time.
7. Run some energy.
8. Check to see that you are grounded and owning the room.
9. Thank your body for being so willing to change and grow.
10. When ready, stand up, stretch, and reverse polarities.

Paradoxically, you can make a very powerful transformation by intentionally placing yourself inside of a picture, then using all of your techniques from "inside" the scene. This is often more powerful than simply blowing the pictures. Once associated into the picture, you can ground, own the room, blow pictures, remove cords, send energy back to others, and recover your own energy. This is called "associating into a picture."

To associate into a picture, you remember a past experience and re-imagine it as if you were actually in the experience in current time. Perceive the picture from inside the scene, not looking at the scene as if it were a photograph, but as if you were there and able to explore the scene by turning your head. Then, from inside both that time and space, you can use your current resources, wisdom, and psychic tools to reorganize your energy, progressively working toward neutrality.

Exercise 36: *Associating into a picture*

1. Rest your awareness in the center of your head, breathe gently into your belly and ground and own the room.

2. Set your crown color to gold for neutrality.
3. Begin creating and destroying roses.
4. Re-imagine a past experience that you want to heal.
5. Associate yourself into the picture. See, hear, and feel yourself back in the event. Breathe.
6. Ground and own the room from within that picture.
7. Patiently allow your breathing to stabilize and gradually become deeper.
8. Create and destroy roses.
9. Remove cords.
10. Send energy back and recover your own energy.
11. Check that you are still breathing gently and deeply into your body.
12. When ready, come out of your picture into current time.
13. Place your past experience in a rose and destroy that rose.
14. Run some energy.
15. Check to see that you are still grounded and owning the room.
16. Thank your body for being willing to change.
17. When ready, stand up, stretch, and reverse polarities.

Suggestions for Further Explorations

1. If you find yourself "lit up" during the day, take the opportunity to blow those pictures in the moment. Since you probably won't be able to take much time, make it simple, and *intend* that you are blowing the pictures lighting up in your aura.
2. If you know you'll be entering a situation that will light you up, such as a big business meeting, heavy traffic, or a test, ground and own the room and begin blowing pictures beforehand. Continue blowing pictures during the situation. Later, take some time to clear any leftover pictures.
3. Set your crown to gold when in heavy traffic, or anytime neutrality is appropriate.

Chapter Seven

The Seven Layers of the Aura

The next stage of your developing self-awareness begins with increasing your ability to perceive and heal the seven layers of your aura. The aura is composed of many different frequencies of energy. These frequencies fall into major ranges or bands of energy which we call "layers" (see figure 7, page 110). In this chapter, the seven layers most closely related to the seven major chakras will be explored.[1]

Layer Descriptions

Each of the layers of the aura grows out of a respective chakra. For example, the first layer grows out of the first chakra, the second layer grows out of the second chakra, and so on. Ideally, the layers surround the entire physical body, each layer expanding a little further out than the preceding one, and interpenetrating each other like Russian nesting dolls. They occupy the same space, though at different frequencies, quite analogous to how radio waves exist within the same space, but at difference frequencies. Each layer vibrates at a little higher frequency than the preceding one, just like their respective chakras.

---

[1]There are both other layers of the aura, and entirely different ways of categorizing and looking at the aura. This seven-layer system is, however, the principal system used in the West today.

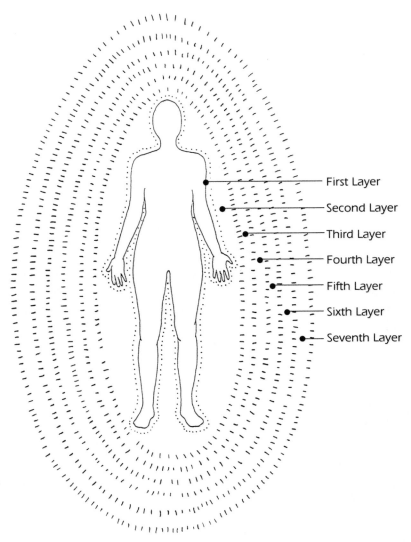

First Layer
Second Layer
Third Layer
Fourth Layer
Fifth Layer
Sixth Layer
Seventh Layer

Figure 7. The seven layers of the aura.

To help you envision how the chakras and layers connect, imagine the layers growing out of the chakras through psychic filaments, similar to the lines of force revealed by placing a magnet under a piece of paper and sprinkling iron filings over it. Similarly, each layer forms a field around the body growing out of the chakra.

Each layer vibrates at the frequency of the related chakra. To gain entry into a layer, therefore, you simply bring your attention to the frequency of the chakra, then move out into its respective layer though the lines of force.[2]

The first layer is the smallest, extending one to three inches beyond the physical body. It grows out of the first chakra and closely follows the contour of your physical body. The second layer, which grows out of your second chakra, extends several inches beyond the first layer and begins to become more egg-shaped. Ideally, each successive layer will extend a little farther out. By the seventh layers, the aura can extend three to five feet beyond the body. Men seem to be comfortable allowing their seventh layers to extend only two to three feet beyond their bodies. Women seem more comfortable allowing their auras to extend three to five feet beyond their physical bodies, because they tend to run their bodies at a higher frequency than men do.

For some, perceiving the layers comes easily, for others it requires more practice. That being said, even if you don't meet your own criteria for "perceiving," you'll still be able to do wonderful healings on your aura with these exercises.

The characteristics of the layers

The layers' characteristics are more abstract than those of the chakras. You can think of the chakras as being yang, more male, compact, action-oriented, and related to how things happen. You can think of the layers as being yin, more female, spacious, and providing a kind of "readout" of your status and relationship with the particular qualities associated with each chakra.

---

[2]This description is simplified for our learning purposes. The aura is a far more complicated and intricate system than will be addressed here. For example, each layer also contains all the chakras.

The first layer, like the first chakra, relates to the health and security of the physical body. Since it is through the body that we manifest, the first layer also relates to manifestation. If your body is in harmony with what you want to manifest, you will get it.

The second layer, like the second chakra, relates to your boundaries and emotions. The third layer relates to concrete intellect, your basic beliefs, your personal power, and your understanding of yourself and others. The fourth layer relates to love and relationships in general: your relationship with yourself, your body, your loved ones, your God of the Heart and your society.

From the fifth layer on, the descriptions are more abstract. The fifth layer pertains to the basic template of your inner identity, your uniqueness. Consequently, it is the layer most related to communication. The sixth layer pertains to systems of beliefs, to nonlinear intellect, group consciousness, higher forms of love, and clairvoyance. The seventh layer is your spiritual template. It contains the creative impulse for your life as a human, as well as the meaning you draw from your human experiences.

The next exercise allows you to familiarize yourself with the location and the energy of each layer. To gain entry into the layers of your aura, find the frequency of each chakra, then from each chakra move out into the corresponding layer. Begin by exploring your first layer and move up, one at a time, to your seventh layer. Remember to go all around your body. Explore front and back, above and below, in each layer.

Exercise 37: *Locating the layers*

1. Resting your awareness in the center of your head, breathe gently and deeply into your belly, and ground and own the room.
2. One at a time, beginning with your first chakra and moving up to the seventh, find the frequency of each chakra, then move your attention into its corresponding layer.

3. Playfully explore each layer, remembering to explore each one in front, behind, above, and below your body.
4. Create and destroy roses.
5. Run Earth and cosmic energy, and replenish your entire aura.
6. Thank your body and check to see that you are still grounded, owning the room, and in the center of your head.
7. When ready, stand up, stretch, and reverse polarities.

Repairing the Boundaries: Good Fences Make Good Neighbors

Next you'll playfully explore and repair the seven boundaries of your auric layers. Repairing your boundaries is a powerful healing you create in your imagination and, even if it seems to be "just imagination," you will begin to heal and own your aura in very profound ways.

For the next exercise, go into the layers of your aura one by one and examine the boundaries, front to back, side to side, top to bottom. For each of the seven layers, see, feel, hear, or imagine something that you'd like to repair on the boundary and then repair it. If you don't find anything apparent that you'd like to change, spend some time smoothing and owning the entire boundary. Contemplating the characteristics of each particular layer can often help you light the boundary up.

As you explore your layers, you may expect that you will find some anomalies. In fact, it would be rare if you found your layers to be in "perfect" order, even if you've already done a lot of self-work. Some common irregularities you may find are rips and holes, "weapons," dents and bumps, rigid boundaries, and often no boundaries at all. As always, you will benefit from blowing pictures while doing the exercise. You might even enjoy blowing pictures as you read the following.

Rips and holes

Rips and holes in your aura are caused by allowing yourself to be invalidated. If you find a rip or hole in your boundary, imagine how you would like to repair it and begin healing and nurturing yourself there. If the hole is not too big, you can pull it together, and use an imaginary needle and thread to sew it closed. If it's a big hole, initially you may only be able to sew it partly closed. If this is the case administer a "psychic poultice," then come back later, pull it in a little further, and put another poultice on it. Or you can create a psychic bandage. This can be playful. You can be as imaginative as you were at age four.

Metaphoric weapons

It is not uncommon to find energies in your aura that resemble weapons. It is most practical to view these as metaphors, rather than as actual weapons. For example, if someone is angry enough, they may unconsciously "stab" you with their energy, and in your mind you may perceive this energy as a dagger. It may look or feel like a dagger to you, but it's actually more often your metaphor for how you experienced the energy.

If you find something that looks like a dagger (or any other kind of weapon) in your layer, just pull it out and drop it down your grounding cord. Blow the pictures that let it into your boundary in the first place, smooth and repair the layer or layers involved, and remember to fill the space with fresh nurturing energy.

No boundaries

Some people have whole layers that have no boundaries at all. In fact, most people will find that some of their outer layers essentially have no boundaries—i.e., the layer doesn't really end, it just thins out and fades away.

Should you find layers with no boundaries, it is often because you didn't believe that you should have, or were entitled to have, boundaries. The inner layers are more closely related to the body; the outer layers are more closely related to psychic experience. People tend to view psychic experience as a type of experience that requires them to have no boundaries.

If you reach a layer that has no boundaries, playfully pat or "hug" it into place and create what you feel is an appropriate boundary. Take your time and give your layer a nice clear boundary all the way around.

Gloria: A good friend uses a delightful technique to repair her boundaries. Recalling the archetype of the Grandmother Spider, Weaver of Worlds, she playfully and gently spins and weaves her boundary repairs out of beautiful gossamer threads.

Advanced student: In the beginning, I had no boundaries. At first, I could almost feel a cold wind fluttering through my tattered aura. I created a wonderful psychic paintbrush, used some "Cosmic Gold" paint from the cosmos, and painted my boundaries back in. I had to repair them often at first, however. Now, I've learned to hold and honor boundaries much more effectively.

Rigid boundaries

Some people may find that they have boundaries that are too tight, too rigid. Rigid beliefs set rigid boundaries. A belief that only the intellect is a reliable guide to decision-making is an example of a rigid belief. A person with such a belief will probably have a dark, static, and poorly formed second layer (emotions) and a rigid third-layer boundary (linear intellect).

If you find rigid boundaries, explore the beliefs relating to that layer and perhaps give your beliefs and the boundary permission to be more adventurous, playful, and flexible.

Dents

Dents in your boundaries are usually caused by a kind of a "energy smack" you received from somebody. Sometimes people unconsciously throw energy at each other to try to get their attention. If you find dents in your layers, imagine a little rubber mallet and playfully knock the boundary back into shape and smooth it out. Grounding, owning the room, and running some energy will help you elude such encounters. And as always, you can create and destroy roses to clear the pictures that let the energy impact your aura.

Bumps

Generally, bumps on the boundary indicate too much energy in the layer, and usually not your own. If you find bumps, first explore and talk to the protruding energy. Then, if you are ready to release it, send the energy back to the person to whom it belongs, while blowing pictures and removing any cords.

Owning your body

A note before you begin exploring and healing your boundaries. Because many of us in this culture do not "own" parts our body, that is, we give little attention to them, there are often portions of the inner layers which lack any coverage. For example, the first layer often fails to include the feet. Pay particular attention to the condition of the layers around your feet, legs, and back. Certain physical complaints, such as cold feet or arthritis, usually correspond to layer and boundary weakness in those areas.

Giving the boundaries a purple border

Sometimes it is helpful to place a purple border around a layer to clarify the boundary. It isn't always necessary to use a purple border, but it can help you perceive your boundaries a little better while working on them, and even help you "own" your boundaries a little better as you work on your aura. You will develop your own sense as to when this is appropriate. It is usually enough to give the seventh layer a border. If you feel you need extra clarity, however, create a purple border for each of your seven layers.

Exercise 38: *Repairing boundaries of the layers*

1. Rest your awareness in the center of your head, breathe gently and deeply into your belly as you ground and own the room.
2. Create and destroy roses.
3. One at a time, beginning with the first and moving to the seventh, explore and repair the boundary of each layer, making sure that it completely surrounds your body. Use your imagination to make any repairs. Continue creating and destroying roses.
4. Come back into the center of your head.
5. Thank your body, and check to see that you are still grounded and owning the room.
6. Run Earth and cosmic energy.
7. When ready, stand up, stretch, and reverse polarities.

How often should you repair your boundaries? We recommend that you explore repairing them a little each day if you can, but at least once a week. Remember, you're setting an intent and addressing a belief system. You're beginning to understand how good fences make good neighbors. That understanding is cumulative and consequently may take a little practice.

Inside the Layers

Now that you've strengthened your boundaries, you'll next want to clean and renovate the interior of the layers. You can imagine improving your layers the same way you might improve the way a room is decorated—if you don't like the way something looks, feels, or sounds, simply change it. It's entirely up to you how you want your layers to look, feel, or sound.

To remove any unwanted energy, colors, sounds, feelings, objects, or whatever you might discover in your aura, create a grounding cord to the center of the Earth, and just let the various energies flow or drop down the cord to be recycled.

How will you know just what to change or improve? Ask yourself if the change will inhibit or encourage the flow of energy in your aura. Allow yourself to play, and trust your intuition. Keep in mind that, with your intent to clear and improve something, you send a message that your body and Deep Self will hear. Things will begin to change for you as you continue to be resourceful.

Colors

If you are visual, you may see colors in your layers. Some may look or feel good, others may not. Usually, murky colors in your aura indicate that someone else's energy is enmeshed with yours. Pulling the murkiness out will free and invigorate your energy. Explore what the colors mean to you. If you don't like the look or feel of a color, you may drain the entire color, or just the part of the color you don't like, by using a little grounding cord. We suggest that you remove most black energy you find in your aura, although, there is a kind of black Great Mother energy that is very nice. You'll come to know the difference with time. White energy usually isn't your energy, so you may want to release any white. If you are unsure about a color, ask it what it is and why it's there.

Empty space

Should you find "empty" space in your aura that seems as if it needs sprucing up, bring in fresh Earth or cosmic energy, filling the space until it feels healthy and playful again. Bring the energy through the chakra out of which the layer grows. For example, if the fourth layer has a void (or, if for any reason you want to bring in a different color), you can bring that color cosmic energy down through the crown chakra to the fourth chakra, and from there out into the fourth layer.

Sounds

If you are auditory and can hear what's going on in your layers, change the sound of the layer. Rhythms can be altered. Tones can be sped up or slowed down, pitched higher or lower, enhanced or, of course, even deleted. To clear a sound out, drain the energy out of it with a grounding cord. Phrases can be run backward, or louder, or softer, until they lose their energy. Or, you can just ask yourself what color a noise vibrates at, and then vacuum out that color. Songs repeating themselves can sometimes be a message for you to release emotional "stuckness." Since the subconscious works through association, songs can also be doorways.

John: A long time ago I had a guide tell me his name was Alfonzo, or something like that. In my youthful arrogance, I felt that was an unacceptably ornate name. The next morning I kept waking up with a song going over and over in my mind. It only took me about two hours to finally make the connection. The words to the song were, "You can call me Al. . . "

If you are kinesthetic

If you are kinesthetic, you'll perceive how your layers feel. Is the layer hot? Is it cold? Is it rough? Is it smooth? Is it flowing? Is it sticky? Is it weak? Is it strong? Allow your layers to flow and feel comfortable in whatever way you'd like them to feel. For example, fill your third layer with the feeling of appropriate power and understanding of yourself and others, your fourth layer with the feeling of emotional warmth, the fifth with the creative power of self expression.

Make changes with love and self-acceptance

If you make your changes from an attitude of play and amusement, it's impossible to get into serious trouble. People who lose their amusement and go ripping through their aura, can invalidate themselves and cause themselves unnecessary difficulty. If you feel an urgency to change, that's okay, just add a little amusement about how invalidating urgency can be. Then take a moment to validate how resourceful you are becoming in recognizing what it is you want to change. Remember, rips and holes in your aura come from only one source, invalidation—either your own or someone else's. In the long run, no one can invalidate you without you invalidating yourself. When you are making these changes, it is helpful to do so from an attitude of love and self-acceptance.

Exercise 39: *Exploring and repairing inside the layers*

1. Resting your awareness in the center of your head, breathe gently and deeply into your belly as you ground and own the room.
2. One by one, beginning with the first chakra and moving up, playfully explore the interior of each layer.
3. Create and destroy roses.
4. Vacuum out any energy that's not yours and make any changes in the layer that please you.
5. Fill each layer up with fresh Earth and/or cosmic energy.
6. Check that you are still grounded, owning the room, and in the center of your head.
7. Release old or excess energy down your grounding cord.
8. Mix Earth and cosmic energy and let it fill your entire aura.
9. When ready, slowly stand up, stretch, and reverse polarities.

Suggestions for Further Explorations

1. Contemplate one of your issues and explore how it looks, sounds, or feels in each layer. Use the tools that feel appropriate to clear and heal it. For example, if you are often rigid about money, explore how your financial beliefs behave in your aura and heal

them. Or, if you allow yourself to be invalidated by others, look for invalidating rips and tears in each layer, heal them, and come into current time with the issue triggering the invalidation.

2. As you work with each layer, explore extending your grounding cord up to the chakra that correlates to the layer. This will help you ground and own the layer. When finished, make certain that your grounding cord returns and is securely fastened to your first chakra.

3. Make up a fantasy for your daily shower to help you clean and own your aura. Let it be easy and playful. For example, imagine healing water washing through each layer of your aura, then effortlessly flowing into the unconditional love of the ocean, where Mother Ocean will recycle the energy for you.

Chapter Eight

Out-of-Body Chakras

There are thousands of chakras, both in the body and outside of the body. You've already explored the seven most significant in-the-body chakras along the spine, together with the newly important hand and foot chakras. Next we'll explore the pertinent "out-of-body" chakras—eight, nine, ten, eleven, and twelve—and their corresponding layers.

By common agreement, there are five major out-of-body chakras.[1] The first three (the eighth, ninth, and tenth) have specific placements and relate to our creativity. The last two (the eleventh and twelfth) are unity chakras. For the out-of-body chakras, the distinction between chakras and layers really begins to break down. The out-of-body chakras are not quite as localized as the in-the-body chakras. They are more hybrid—half layers, half chakras. As you become more psychic, you will probably begin to respond just as much to these outer layers as you do to their corresponding chakras, much more so than you will be likely to do with the in-the-body chakras and their respective layers.

---

[1]There is much more variation in systems for out-of-body chakras than there is for in-the-body chakras. The system presented here focuses most strongly on the human experience. It was suggested by the work of Petey Stevens in *Opening Up to Your Psychic Self* (Albany, CA: Nevertheless Press, 1983), pp. 69–80.

Out-of-Body Chakras:
Placement and Description

With the out-of-body chakras, as with many psychic concepts, it's best to take a flexible, rather than a literal, approach. For example, each of the first three out-of-body chakras has an upper chakra and a corresponding lower chakra. These chakras are referenced by how far they are above your head or below your feet (see figure 8, page125). If you want to drive yourself crazy, ask yourself what happens if you raise one foot quite a bit higher than the other? Where is your eighth chakra then? Well, it may move, or it may not. After you've become thoroughly familiar with each chakra's normal placement, you'll find the chakra easily, regardless of your body position.

The first of the out-of-body chakras is the eighth chakra. The upper eighth is a foot above your crown, and the lower eighth is one foot below your feet. The upper ninth is three feet above your crown, and the lower ninth is three feet below your feet. The upper tenth is one foot above the upper ninth (that is, four feet above your crown), the lower tenth is one foot below your lower ninth (that is four feet below your feet).

The eleventh and twelfth chakras move out of placement and into pure metaphor, pure symbol. They are everywhere. To connect with the eleventh chakra, imagine yourself going out through every cell of your body into All That Is, where you are in unity with All That Is, yet have your own identity. As an individual, you are unified with everything. To enter the twelfth chakra, let go of your attention on "you" and attend only to the experience of unity. The focus of your attention on unity is a matter of degree. It doesn't mean that you black out or go into a bliss state. You merely focus on the energy of unity, the frequency and state of unity.

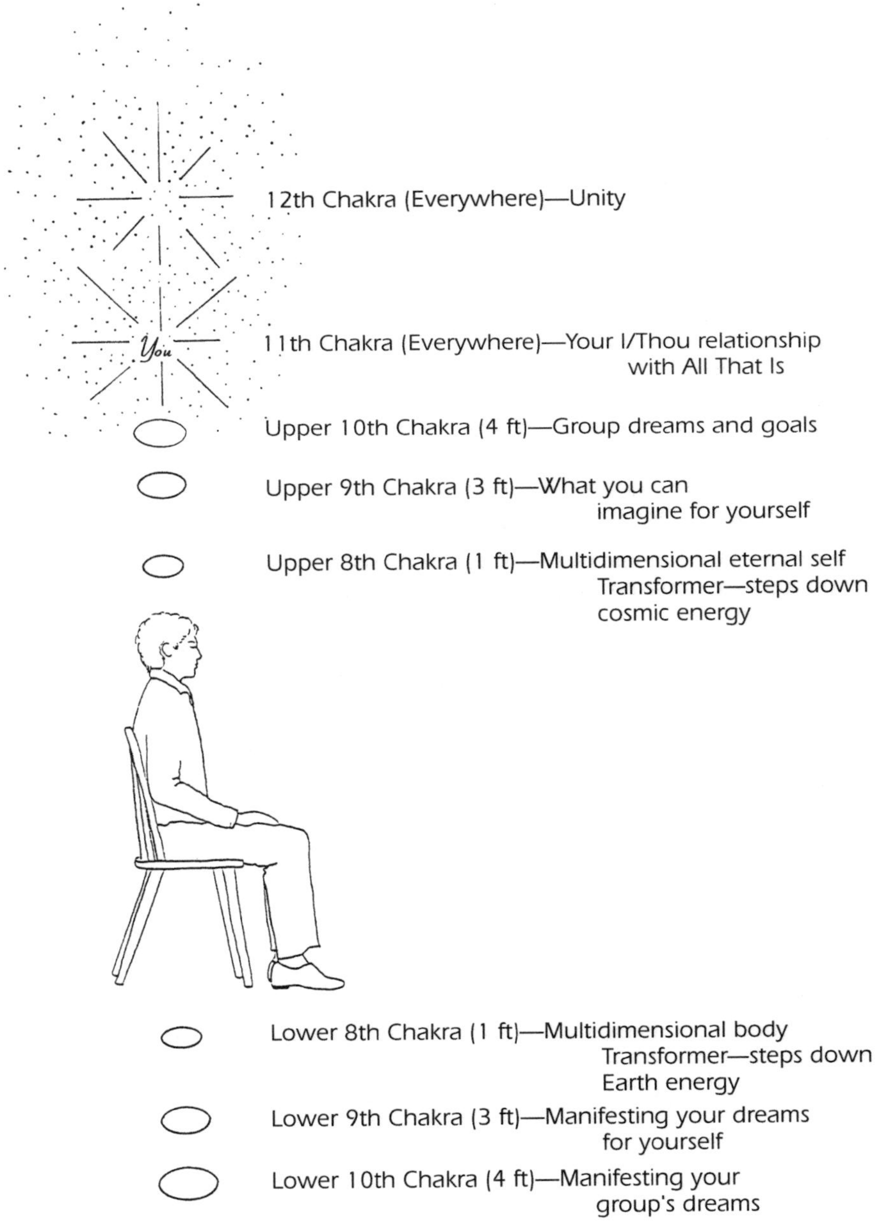

12th Chakra (Everywhere)—Unity

11th Chakra (Everywhere)—Your I/Thou relationship
with All That Is

Upper 10th Chakra (4 ft)—Group dreams and goals

Upper 9th Chakra (3 ft)—What you can
imagine for yourself

Upper 8th Chakra (1 ft)—Multidimensional eternal self
Transformer—steps down
cosmic energy

Lower 8th Chakra (1 ft)—Multidimensional body
Transformer—steps down
Earth energy

Lower 9th Chakra (3 ft)—Manifesting your dreams
for yourself

Lower 10th Chakra (4 ft)—Manifesting your
group's dreams

Figure 8. The "out-of-body" chakras.

The eighth chakra:
information access and energy transformer

The eighth chakra is where your past life, future life, and probable life information is found. It is your multidimensional self (upper eighth) and your mulitdimensional body (lower eighth).[2]

It's also your transformer chakra, stepping down energies from the cosmos and the planet so that your body can run them safely and smoothly. As with a transformer in your house, the current comes in at a certain level, then is appropriately lessened so that it doesn't short out your appliances. The upper eighth chakra steps down the cosmic energy to a level that your body can run safely and comfortably. The lower eighth chakra steps down Earth energy to a level your body can run safely and comfortably.

The ninth chakra: the limits of your imagination

The ninth chakra contains the scope of your personal dreams. Not to be confused with sleeping dreams, it refers to the limits of your imagination for yourself. It's not necessarily what you can or will actually do, but what you can allow yourself to imagine for yourself. The lower ninth chakra facilitates the manifestation of those dreams for yourself. You cannot manifest something for yourself that you cannot first imagine.

John: Years ago, one of my friends, a very bright, self-confident and successful nurse, was clearing her out-of-body chakras when she realized, "I could have been a doctor!" It just hadn't been part of her worldview as she was growing up that a woman could be a doctor. Consequently, though amply gifted to be either a nurse or a doctor, she hadn't even been able to consider which she would prefer. That's a ninth chakra restriction.

---

[2]According to recent channelings of an emerging version of Seth (called Mataji) through John.

The tenth chakra: your group affiliations and agreements

The tenth chakra is a lot like the ninth chakra, except that it has to do with your group relationships, what your group can dream and manifest for itself. The human race is the most obvious group that we are all a part of. You will find your connection to the hopes and dreams of the human race in the tenth chakra. In fact, global healings often take place in the upper and lower tenth.

The tenth chakra also relates to any particular group affiliations, such as church, work, charities, or environmental groups. Since the upper tenth chakra is what you can imagine and dream of as a group, what is permissible and what is not permissible, you'll very often find your group agreements in the tenth. The lower tenth chakra facilitates the manifestation of your group's dreams and desires into physicality.

The eleventh and twelfth chakras: unity

Since the eleventh and twelfth chakras are unity chakras, they tend to defy description. Consider them as mediators of your relationship with All That Is, or the Void.

Locating your out-of-body chakras

You can imagine the first seven chakras as a ladder, each successive chakra going up in frequency to direct and show you the way to the out-of-body chakras. In the following exercise, you will locate the out-of-body chakras—hear them, feel them, see them.

Exercise 40: *Locating your out-of-body chakras*

1. Resting your awareness in the center of your head, breathe gently and deeply into your belly as you ground and own the room.
2. Begin creating and destroying roses.
3. Run about ten times as much cosmic energy as Earth energy.

4. Using the chakras as a ladder, find the frequency of each chakra and climb, one at a time, from the first to the seventh chakra.
5. Move your attention one foot above your crown and say hello to and explore your upper eighth chakra.
6. Next move your attention one foot below your feet and say hello to and explore your lower eighth chakra.
7. Playfully continue to create and destroy roses.
8. Proceed to three feet above your crown and say hello to and explore your upper ninth chakra.
9. Move your attention to three feet below your feet and say hello to and explore your lower ninth chakra.
10. Move your attention to four feet above your crown and say hello to and explore your upper tenth chakra.
11. Move your attention to four feet below your feet and say hello to and explore your lower tenth chakra.
12. For the eleventh chakra, go through every cell in your body, out into union, and say hello to yourself in union with All That Is.
13. For the twelfth chakra, let go of your focus on yourself and focus only on unity itself.
14. Check to see that you are still in the center of your head, grounded and owning the room.
15. Run ten times as much cosmic energy as Earth energy.
16. Say hello to and thank your body.
17. When ready, stand up, stretch, and reverse polarities.

Cleaning your out-of-body chakras

In the next exercise, you will clean and replenish your out-of-body chakras in the same manner that you cleaned and replenished your in-the-body chakras. For each chakra, create and destroy roses, vacuum energy, and remove cords. Though it may seem unlikely, you will probably find cords in your out-of-body chakras, even in your unity chakras. You may not be able to see or feel them very easily, but they are usually there.

Begin by cleaning out your upper eighth, then your lower eighth chakra. Then clean the upper and lower ninth, and so on, all the way to, and including, your twelfth chakra. If you keep in mind what each chakra represents, it may help you to light up any pictures, energy, or cords there.

Student: I enjoy working with my out-of-body chakras to explore my personal beliefs and limitations. For instance, I discovered a kind of piously inspired unworthiness in my upper ninth that was very destructive to my ability to open up to abundance. It was very interesting to realize the uncountable ways in which I had allowed it to block me.

Exercise 41: *Cleaning out-of-body chakras*

1. Resting your awareness in the center of your head, breathe gently and deeply into your belly as you ground and own the room.
2. Using the chakras as a ladder, find the frequency of each chakra and move, one at a time, from the first to the seventh chakra.
3. One foot above your crown, see, hear, or feel the upper eighth chakra.
4. Near your upper eighth chakra, create and destroy roses.
5. Create a vacuum-cleaner rose, remove energy, then destroy that rose.
6. Remove cords.
7. Fill your upper eighth chakra with a color of your choice.
8. Move to the lower eighth chakra and repeat the clearing and replenishing process.
9. In the same manner, proceed through all the remaining out-of-body chakras.

10. When finished, check to see that your consciousness is in the center of your head, and that you are still grounded and owning the room.
11. Say hello to and thank your body.
12. Run ten times as much gold cosmic as fresh Earth energy.
13. When ready, stand up, stretch, and reverse polarities.

Suggestions for Further Explorations

1. Explore your relationship to each of your out-of-body chakras. For instance, identify and clear any blocks restricting the flow of Earth or cosmic energy in the eighth chakra. For the ninth chakra, reflect on what you can dream for yourself and bring those dreams up to date. For the tenth chakra, have a conversation with the planet about your hopes and dreams for humanity. In the eleventh chakra, continue exploring your relationship with unity, and for the twelfth chakra, explore unity itself. Remember to make certain that you are still grounded and owning the room after working with your out-of-body chakras.
2. Create a meditation to explore and clear any limiting rules from your past group affiliations in your upper and lower tenth chakra.

Chapter Nine

Communicating with Your Healing Guide

Your relationship with your healing guide is precious beyond knowing and, like all relationships, grows richer with care and nurturing. By opening up your receptivity and availability to spirit, you make your relationship with your guides more playful, more magical, more practical, more intimate, and more of a conscious collaboration. The following exercises are designed to help you open and cultivate a fuller, more conscious relationship with your healing guide.

For many, this will be an introduction to the awesome adventure of collaborative consciousness. For those of you who already have a working relationship with your guides, these exercises will nourish and broaden that relationship in increasingly practical and sublime ways.

In this system, we define any being or influence that can whisper in your ear as a guide. So, along with your beneficial spirit guides, any energy in your aura from which you accept guidance, past or present (such as energy from a parent or teacher) acts, in a sense, as a guide. All the techniques in this book have been designed to help you maintain healthy psychic boundaries and your own authority in your body and aura. The techniques help you determine who you are within your relationships, what is your energy and what is not your energy, how to own your body and aura, and how to run your own energy. In the same way, as you open to a more conscious relationship with spirit, you will continue to maintain healthy psychic boundaries and seniority, you will continue to maintain your uniqueness, and you will continue to identify and own your aura.

How will you contact your healing guide? You can use the following techniques with a playful and open frame of mind and simply state your intent, your wish to open up your relationship with your guides. Let them know you're ready to play. It's good to remember, regardless of whether or not you consciously see, feel, or hear your guides in the beginning, that they are with you. You may have to clear some energy and blow some pictures to help you perceive their presence, but we encourage you to presuppose (or at least be open to the possibility) that you are communicating with guides. Such a presupposition will quicken the development of your conscious relationship and create the space for the relationship to grow.

The Healing Guide and the Rose

The next meditation will help you become acquainted with your healing guide.

Everyone has at least several guides. When you ask for your healing guide, you are asking for one of your guides that is skilled in healing to step forward. How do you know the guide is well-intentioned? Usually that's not a problem. You have enough help so that someone with good intentions will be able to step forward. More importantly, all these techniques are set up to make certain you know how to maintain your boundaries, your separation. All the techniques you have learned will help you eventually separate from unhelpful influences. If you have any doubts, you can delay working with guides until later, or until you find a personal teacher to help you.

Ground and own the room, then create a rose about ten feet in front of you. Creating a rose makes it a lot easier to communicate with your guide because it gives you a place to direct your communication. Invite your healing guide onto the rose and have a leisurely chat.

Of course, this chat is telepathic, not vocal. At first it may seem as if you are making up the conversation. Give yourself time to grow in your discernment. The imagination is the doorway through which psychic information flows. As time goes by you will come to know what comes from another and what comes from yourself.

You can talk about anything you'd like, though we suggest you keep it simple in the beginning. Just take your time and get to know your guide. Speak in the same way you might speak with anyone you've desired to meet and have at last met. Some people like to ask for a name. You could ask your guide to send you some energy so you can feel it. (Be certain to send it back when you are through.) You could ask him or her if they have something to tell you. There are no rules. Just enjoy your time together.

When you are through talking, thank your guide and then ask it to go back behind your aura—not *in* your aura, but behind it about six feet. Your guide will move into another dimension. Don't worry, it won't get bored. Guides can be in 20 billion places at the same time, and yet they will be available the next time you want to talk.

Some spirit guides will know to move back behind your aura, while others may need to be reminded. In the past, many of our guides have had to move inside our auras to get our attention. Now, you are learning to communicate with them by having them remain outside of your aura. Paradoxically, you will have a healthier, enhanced relationship with your guides by maintaining your boundaries. After they have moved behind you, make certain to separate your energy from theirs.

Making your separations

Consciously separating from your guide is easy. Just repeat five times to yourself, "I have a physical body, and you are of spirit," or something similar. You might want to make up your own phrase to set your boundaries.

Telepathic communications

Exercise 42 may help some to begin receiving telepathic communications from their guides. For others, the ability may come on-line more slowly, over a period of several months. In either case, we suggest that you playfully open up to that possibility.

Guide names

Names are often nice to use in communicating with guides. Guides don't really have names in the same sense that we do. One person's name for a guide might be different from another person's name for the same guide. People can have the same guide and use different names because the name is a metaphor for a relationship that they have with that guide.

How guides may appear to you

We usually see guides as light. Some of you who are very visual will see them with specific features and clothing. These are simply just two different ways of perceiving them; neither is superior to the other. We would encourage you to avoid taking what you see too literally. What you see may not be all of who that guide is.

Exercise 42: *Your healing guide and the rose*

1. Resting your awareness in the center of your head, breathe gently and deeply into your belly as you ground and own the room.
2. Run some Earth and cosmic energy.
3. Clear your clairvoyance with cosmic blue and gold energy.
4. Create and destroy roses.
5. Create a rose ten feet in front of you.
6. Invite your healing guide to come onto your rose.
7. Enjoy communicating with your healing guide.
8. When through, thank your healing guide.

9. Ask your guide to go behind your aura, then destroy the rose you used for the exercise.
10. Separate from your guide.
11. Create and destroy roses, and replenish your aura.
12. Check that you are still grounded and owning the room.
13. When ready, stand up, stretch, and reverse polarities.

Note: Since it's so important for you to know how to maintain clear boundaries with your guide, we recommend that you practice Exercise 42 until you are certain you know how to separate from your guide before you explore Exercise 44, Healing with your healing guide.

Communicating with Your Healing Guide

We want to encourage you to ask your healing guide to come onto a rose at least a couple of times a week so that you can chat and continue to become more familiar. Even if you don't see, feel, or hear your guides clearly at first, just intend that they are there. Use all of your senses to develop communication. There's no right or wrong way. The whole purpose is to build your relationship, gradually, safely, with you deciding just how much intimacy you want.

Healing guide fantasy

For the next exercise, travel in your mind's eye to a place of your creation, where you and your healing guide can meet and talk at leisure.[1] Create your own special place just for the two of you, a magical place that you can visit any time you'd like. Allow yourself to become very relaxed, then imagine yourself going out through white light to your fantasy place.

---

[1] Whether you are consciously aware of it or not, sending part of yourself out through your mind's eye will result in some of your energy traveling to the astral, or some other plane.

Walk down a path through the woods until you come to a beautiful beach where you stroll along the shoreline with your guide. Or go to a concert where you both listen to beautiful music. Or simply imagine a wonderful flat rock where you can just hang out with your guide in the sun for a while. It's that simple. Just create a fantasy that's to your liking, simple or grand, there are no rules. When you're finished, thank your guide, separate, ground, own the room, and, as with any time you send part of yourself on a fantasy through your mind's eye, be sure to bring all of your energy back when you return.[2]

There are a number of ways to get to a white-light level for this fantasy. Again, use your imagination. You could go through a door into a room of white-light, or onto an elevator that takes you to a white-light level and brings you back down, or you could simply surround yourself in white light. Another favorite is to imagine yourself going up a white-light fireman's pole. When you're finished, you can just slide down out of the white-light level. Again, it's just play.

Exercise 43: *Healing guide fantasy*

1. Resting your awareness in the center of your head, breathe gently and deeply into your belly as you ground and own the room.
2. Run Earth and cosmic energy.
3. Clear your clairvoyance.
4. Create and destroy roses.
5. Imagine yourself at a white-light level.
6. Create your fantasy in which you meet your healing guide.

---

[2]Bring back all your energy that "belongs." John has seen some people pull some of their dream body, which resides in and belongs in other, more multifaceted dimensions, back into their physical body. That would interfere with setting the physical body at the right frequency.

7. Communicate with your healing guide.
8. When finished, thank your healing guide and ask him or her to go behind your aura.
9. Put a picture of your fantasy in a rose and destroy it.
10. Come out of the white-light level by grounding, by clearing and grounding any white-light out of your aura, and running green Earth and gold cosmic energy.
11. Separate from your healing guide.
12. Create and destroy roses.
13. Check to see that you're still grounded and owning the room.
14. When ready, stand up, stretch, and reverse polarities.

Letting Your Guide Heal Through Your Hand Chakras

Collaborating with your healing guide to do healings on others is a lot of fun. In the next exercise, you learn how to invite your healing guide into your hand chakras to do healings for yourself and others. Healing also provides you with another wonderful way to increase your psychic abilities, both through the intimate interaction with your guide and through the greater ease in perceiving energy when an energy field is lit up and moving.

It is important to understand that you will be using your guide's energy to do the healings and not your own. People using their own energy to do healings can experience loss of energy and boundaries. There is margin for error here. Some of your energy will inevitably creep into your healings. That is why you make your separations and bring your energy back. By intending to use the guide's energy, you maintain sufficient clarity for safe healing.

Offering your hand chakras to your guide provides it with a physical entry point, a frequency transformer that will enable your guide to give healings in ways he or she could not otherwise do without your physical collaboration.

Inflicting a healing

Before you begin, we feel it is important to give an overview
of what we consider to be a healthy and safe healing practice,
an overview that will help you avoid falling into seriousness
and doing what we call "inflicting a healing." Personally, we
like to do spiritual healings because they're fun, exciting, and
adventurous. They are a way of sharing, and appropriately
connecting, with people in a very intimate and collaborative
way. We learn a lot about other people and especially
ourselves.

Gloria: John often jokes, "In a sane world, we'd pay people to
let us heal them because of the tremendous amount of growth
it stirs in ourselves." As I do a healing on someone, my
matching pictures "light up" and provide me with the opportunity to clear some of my own issues. It's fascinating to see
what each person reveals to me about myself. Every healing I
give someone else is an adventure in self-discovery.

The core of graceful healing requires being as open to healing one's self as one is to healing others. Healing somebody
without changing yourself is unnatural and covertly coercive.
This follows from the fact that we create our own reality according to our beliefs. For a person to heal another without
changing themselves is to deny their interconnection and relationship. Such an unrelated healing would distort the natural order of events, creating a dichotomy between the healer
and the recipient and imposing a viewpoint or identity on
them—in other words, "laying a trip" on them. When you
recognize that in healing someone, you are healing yourself,
and you attend to as much of your own process as possible,
then the healing is a bilateral process. It is a mutual process,
integrated with the whole, with the Tao, with the natural
order of events.

When we are engaged in healing for adventure and
growth, we are exploring whatever happens. We can recognize that those receiving the healings accept them on their

own behalf and that it's their decision, not ours, whether or not they get healed. It's a choice, and all choices are sacred. So, humor and adventure help us to keep what we consider a more appropriate perspective.

John: You can think of healing someone as the breeze that blows the ripened apple off the tree. If you force the healing, you can get the apple off the tree, it'll just be premature and sour.

You won't be and needn't be impeccable in doing just the right amount of healing, but you can explore your healing abilities with as much amusement and integrity as possible. As you become more effective and more knowledgeable as a healer, you become less "klutzy" about it. Initially, you will, at times, overstep the proper bounds, but if you do your healing with a good heart and with playfulness, your healings will work out. If you stay in amusement, you won't become powerful enough to harm until you also become more capable of discerning what constitutes giving a healing and what constitutes inflicting a healing.

Healing others with your healing guide

To do a healing on someone with your healing guide, have the recipient sit in a chair around which you, the healer, can move freely. Begin blowing pictures. If your recipients are familiar with the techniques, you can have them ground and own the room. If not, simply brief them on how to ground. Then, suggest that they relax and just be open to the healing.

As the healer, stand behind the chair, and go into amusement. Ground and own the room, close your second chakra down to 10 percent to help you stay clear as to what is your energy, what is your guide's, and what is the person's you are healing. Relax into a neutral, amused space and place each hand about a foot from each of the recipient's ears. Open your hand chakras wide and invite your healing guide into them. Take a moment to sense your guide's presence. Then, without touching the recipient, allow your guide to direct your hands around the recipient's body as the guide gives them a healing. Remind yourself that you are not doing the healing. You may watch psychically, and usually will, as your perceptual abilities grow, but it isn't necessary. Even when you become very clairvoyant, your guide will sometimes be able to heal more, or more rapidly, than you can see.

When you are finished with the healing, thank your guide, and ask it to move back behind your aura. Then separate from both your guide and the person you healed by noting five physical differences, such as clothing, height, or hair color. This gently brings your attention to the differences and that attention will automatically contribute to clarity. We suggest that you explain to the recipient how to separate from you as well, by noting five physical differences between the two of you. You don't have to agree on the differences. Run some energy and make sure you are grounded and owning the room. Then, about thirty minutes later, check your intuition to see that you are fully separated.

Your guide's subtle energy will direct your hands

Your guide will indicate what you are to do with your hands. His or her energy will probably feel very subtle, like warmth or coolness on your hands. Or like a slight breeze or pull. Sometimes it feels like a little cobweb string that would break if you pulled on it very hard.

The hardest part of doing a healing

The hardest part of the healing isn't getting started; it is knowing when to stop. Most often, you'll be able to tell when your healing guide is finished by the cessation of the energy flow through your hands. The energy will just stop. But while you are learning, there may be times when you are not sure, because the energy is often so subtle. If you are uncertain, you can test it. Slowly and gently begin to move your hands away. If the energy is still moving, you may feel a subtle pull or pulse. Another technique is to create a "yes/no" gauge and ask, "Is the healing over?"[3] (See figure 6, page 94.) Or you can create a red-light/green-light signal. Use whatever metaphor you want that may help. Perhaps the most important suggestion, however, is to accept that it may be hard to tell in the beginning, and remembering your amusement, end the healing when it just feels like it's "time" to you.

When finished, ask your guide to move outside of your aura

When the healing is finished, thank your guide and ask him or her to go back behind your aura. As we said before, you needn't worry. Your guide won't get bored. Guides hang out in some other dimensions where they stay busy. Only some of their attention need ever be on you. They will be available the next time you want to do a healing or just to chat.

Be sure to ground and to make your separations between yourself and the person you healed, and between yourself and your guide as well.

Blowing pictures during the healing

By now, you understand that blowing pictures is not merely a mechanical act; you blow pictures with the intention of changing and transforming yourself. So, if you are exploding your own pictures during the healing, you are honoring your own process and honoring the truth that you, too, must change during a healing.

Permission

Do you have to ask permission to give a healing? "Yes," is the simple answer. Under certain circumstances, however, we feel that's not the right question. Most of the time, permission and lack of it will be obvious, but it's the subtleties of the underlying energy of the situation that we encourage you to examine

---

[3]Using a gauge in this way was first brought to our attention by friend and NLP maven, Art Giser.

closely. Sometimes people will come up to you and beg, "Oh, please heal me, please heal me." In effect, to heal some of these people would be inflicting a healing, because, even though they say they want to be healed, part of them, enough of them, doesn't want to be healed. So, we feel the more appropriate questions are, "Does their energy *itself* seem to want a healing?" and, "Do I want to give a healing?" Both questions must be answered yes for a healing to be appropriate.

No hands-on healing

In this system, we recommend that you do not do "hands-on" healing until you understand how to avoid leaving programming or your "best intentions" in the other person's aura.[4] This is a nice safety feature to learn, as it honors the other person's process and boundaries. Sometimes, even with the best of intentions, you can leave your programming in someone's aura. Some systems intentionally place thought-forms and programming into someone's aura. In this system, we do our best to avoid programming others. We try to avoid assuming we know what is best for another. We're attempting to free and open up possibilities, not to narrow them.

Obviously, if you're a body worker, you are touching people all the time. In such a case, we encourage you to go ahead and explore working with your healing guide and to become more aware of programming. We're certainly not suggesting that your programming would be intentional, or even conscious, but, unless body workers are careful, it is all too easy to unintentionally program a client.

John: That doesn't mean, for example, that I never program. It's not intentional, but it does happen. I am human. We can never control all our behavior and we all have opinions which

---

[4]Programming is a collection of tiny interrelated pictures which create strong tendencies and narrow the recipient's flexibility. You can program someone whether you touch them or not, it's just easier to program them while touching.

carry strong, though unrecognized, implications for those with whom we interact.

I had a sobering experience in my advanced class once. I asked the students to find and remove any of my programming in their space. I was chagrined to see how much better they looked when they had removed it!

It's a good idea to stay amused about your inevitable lack of total control. Someone who gets excessively serious about not programming others will still program them. They will just inadvertently put "invisibility" around their programming so they don't see themselves doing it. That just makes it harder for the recipient to find and clear the programming.

Maintain your neutrality while healing

Should the person receiving the healing become over-wrought and emotional during a healing, compassionately validate the experience, while staying as neutral as possible. Both are necessary; validating their experience, even if it is distorted, helps them recognize their own experience as the starting point for change, and your neutrality avoids enmeshment. Becoming enmeshed can cause you to fall into "seriousness" and to impose the healing rather than offer it. Becoming enmeshed can also increase the possibility of your drawing the person's energy into your own aura, especially into your second chakra. Should you, as the healer, become emotional, remember with amusement that doing a healing will light you up. Blow your own pictures, own the room, and run energy.

The happy healer

We are often asked why the guides give healings. They like to have fun too. They give to us joyously and celebrate healing as an opportunity to express their fondness and tenderness toward us.

John: I knew a woman with a guide who would come in and start healing with the enthusiasm of a puppy. The whole

144 • Basic Psychic Development

room would just fill with its enjoyment and its enthusiasm while doing the healing. I used to call that guide "The Happy Healer." That's why they do it; because it's fun.

Exercise 44: *Healing with your healing guide*

1. Resting your awareness in the center of your head, breathe gently and deeply into your belly as you ground and own the room.
2. Create and destroy roses for the pictures that light up.
3. Close down your second chakra to 10 percent and move into a neutral, amused state.
4. Open your hand chakras all the way.
5. Ask your healing master to come into your hand chakras.
6. Remembering your amusement, and without touching the person you're healing, allow your healing master to guide your hands around the person's body.
7. Continue to create and destroy roses.
8. When you're done, say to yourself, "The healing is over."
9. Thank your guide and ask it to move back behind your aura.
10. Make your separations from both your healing master and the person you've healed.
11. Send the person's energy back, and bring your energy back using the satellite-dish rose.
12. Check that you are still grounded and owning the room.
13. Fill your aura with Earth and cosmic energy.
14. Stretch, pat your body, and reverse polarities.

Heal yourself also

We encourage you also to bring your guide in to do healings on yourself. Guides enjoy it. It's play to them. Sit down, ground and own the room, and let your healing guide come into your hands to do a healing on your body and aura, just as you let it use your hands to heal other people. Or, you can invite your guide into your aura, go into a "giving-to-yourself" state, and let it work on you. You can sit back and enjoy it. You can ask your healing guide to do a healing on you every day if you like. At the end, make sure you do your separations.

Learn how to separate well

Until you are more experienced, we encourage you to limit your healings on others. Do them two or three times a week at most. Beginners often fail to separate well enough and can pull a lot of the other people's energy into their space. People who don't make their separations well can require a couple of days before their unconscious mind returns the energies to the proper person.[5] With experience, you will make your separations quickly and well. With experience you can do healings as frequently as your intuition tells you is appropriate.

Healing over distance

We are often asked, "Can I just send a healing to someone who isn't present?" Yes, by all means. But don't assume that everyone wants a healing. You can go up to the God-of-the-Heart level and ask to be sure. And, of course, even with absentee healings, you want to separate from the person when you are through.

Whatever can go right, will

There are many ways in which your guide enjoys nurturing and supporting you. For example, if you have a negotiation or a presentation coming up, you can ask your guide to clear energy and ground the space, consistent, of course, with everyone's free will. Guides will help you clear your aura, interpret your dreams, and they love to meditate with you.

---

[5]Energy is often unconsciously sorted out and returned to the proper person. Conscious awareness just allows you to sort out the energy more effectively and thoroughly.

They can help you find lost objects. At times, they may suggest a certain book for you to study, and sometimes even where to find them.

Gloria: One morning my guide suggested that I read Anodea Judith's book, *Eastern Body, Western Mind*. I called many stores, but no one in town had it in stock. My guide told me that one particular store *did* have it, even though a very accommodating clerk had spent ten minutes searching for it when I had inquired earlier. So, I went to the store and searched the New Age section myself. All of her other books were there, but not that one. My guide suggested I search the philosophy section. An exhaustive, but unsuccessful, search left me standing in the philosophy section perplexed and wondering if I had misunderstood. All of a sudden, I could feel my guide's exuberant joy and enthusiasm all around me, then my back became very hot. It felt so much like the book was right behind me that I couldn't help but laugh out loud. I turned around and there it was.

Occasionally, people express concern about asking guides to help us with the mundane.

John: I like to say, "Whatever can go right, will." For example, when we understand that we've got all this help around us, we notice that, as soon as our guides can find a way to give appropriate help, they will. They're like a terrific running-back looking for a hole in the line. As soon as they see just a glimmer of daylight (opportunity), they go for it. If we'd only let them. We don't have to do all the work, we don't have to meet them halfway, but, we do have to meet them, because it's our lives, and our decisions are supposed to govern our creative life explorations. With that provision, if they can possibly help you, they will.

That reminds me of the time when I and two of my Buddhist friends were driving around looking for a parking space, and I said, "Gee, if I'd remembered sooner, I would have had my parking guide prepare a space for us." And they said,

"Would you use a guide for something like that?"—the implication being, why would I use my karma for something that trivial. The answer is that guides enjoy it and I need all the practice I can get. Far from using up anything, by interacting with and collaborating with my guides, I am building skills.

The more you communicate with and practice with your guides, the easier it becomes, not only to find a parking space, but more importantly, to increase and hone your intuitive skills. Through practice, you increase the naturalness and familiarity with which you can communicate with your guide, and you give yourself the flexibility and freedom to be more adventurous and playful.

It is our sense that the New Age is about the development of a new kind of identity, a set of skills having to do with a certain openness, and a certain lovingness. We feel it has nothing to do with "perfection," although it does eventually lead to the ability both to be in unity with all things great and small and to be individuated and skillful enough to take part joyously in the dance of life.

Suggestions for Further Explorations

1. If you ever find an unhelpful guide in your aura, blow pictures, remove cords, and ask your healing guide to escort them to their next appropriate step (which, of course, will be outside of your aura). Then replenish your aura with your own energy.

2. The next time you take a trip, practice asking your guides travel-related questions. For example, you could ask what route would be faster or safer. Or what restaurant will have the best foods and service. Or for help in finding a parking place. It may take you awhile to get "clear" suggestions. Play, and explore the information you perceive. If necessary, use a gauge to help you identify other people's energy in your answers and use your techniques to clear out what is not you.

In Conclusion

We hope that you find, as we do, that your skills grow rapidly, often veering in unexpected and exciting directions. As you continue to deepen your intuition and aura-awareness, we encourage you to remember to play. And please remember, it is better to be resourceful than to have all sorts of resources. We wish you well.

Suggested Reading

Andreas, Connirae and Tamara. *Core Transformation: Reaching the Wellspring Within*. Moab, UT: Real People Press, 1994.

Bolton, Robert, Ph.D. *People Skills*. New York: Simon and Schuster, 1979.

Choa, Kok Sui. *Pranic Healing*. York Beach, ME: Samuel Weiser, 1990.

Choquette, Sonia. *Your Heart's Desire: Instructions for Creating the Life You Really Want*. New York: Three Rivers Press, 1997.

Das, Lama Surya. *Awakening the Buddha Within: Eight Steps to Enlightenment*. New York: Broadway Books, 1997.

Dilts, Robert, Tim Hallbom, and Suzi Stuart. *Beliefs: Pathways to Health and Well-Being*. Portland, OR: Metamorphous Press, 1990. (Advanced study)

Friedlander, John and Cynthia Pearson. *The Practical Psychic*. York Beach, ME: Samuel Weiser, 1991.

Gawain, Shakti. *Creative Visualization*. New York: Bantam Books, 1982.

Horn, Sam. *Tongue Fu! How to Deflect, Disarm, and Defuse any Verbal Conflict*. New York: St. Martin's Griffin, 1996.

Johari, Harish. *Chakras: Energy Centers of Transformation*. Rochester, VT: Destiny Books, 1987.

Judith, Anodea. *Eastern Body, Western Mind: Psychology and the Chakra System as a Path to the Self*. Berkeley, CA: Celestial Arts, 1996.

LaBorde, Genie Z. *Influencing with Integrity*. Palo Alto, CA: Syntony Publishing, 1987.

Myss, Caroline, Ph.D. *Anatomy of the Spirit: The Seven Stages of Healing*. New York: Harmony Books, 1996.

Roberts, Jane. *The Nature of Personal Reality*. New York: Bantam Books, 1974.

Stevens, Petey. *Opening Up To Your Psychic Self.* Albany, CA: Nevertheless Press, 1983.

Wallace, Amy and Bill Henkin. *The Psychic Healing Book.* Oakland, CA: Wingbow Press, 1978.

Index

JOHN FRIEDLANDER grew up in Georgia and began his metaphysical education during his college days. He has degrees from Duke University and Harvard Law School. He spent time in India, studied with Lewis Bostwick at the Berkley Psychic Institute in California and joined Jane Roberts' Seth class. He practiced law from 1974–1989, but began to teach classes in psychic awareness in 1982. Today he concentrates on teaching students about new dimensions and is available for private readings in addition to his seminar schedule. John and his wife currently live in Saline, MI. He can be reached at Fried2SaHi@aol.com.

GLORIA HEMSHER began her studies in yoga and meditation in the early 70s, and lived for several years in one of Swami Muktananda's ashrams. In 1973 she became a professional photographer, and then managed a media production center and taught photography. After completing John Friedlander's psychic awareness courses, and following several years of personal work with John and his version of Seth, she began her new career. She teaches psychic development and gives private readings. She lives in Cincinnati, OH with her husband and two children. She can be reached at HemsherGlo@aol.com.